CIRENCESTER
A History and Guide

JEAN
WELSFORD

ALAN SUTTON
1987

Alan Sutton Publishing Limited
Brunswick Road · Gloucester

First published 1987

British Library Cataloguing in Publication Data

Welsford, Jean
Cirencester : a history and guide.
1. Cirencester (Gloucestershire)—History
I. Title
942.4'17   DA690.C61

ISBN 0-86299-386-3

Cover illustration: The Shambles, Market Place prior to 1830
clearance. Courtesy Bingham Library

Typesetting and origination by
Alan Sutton Publishing Limited
Printed in Great Britain

Contents

To Alan

Acknowledgements

The permission of the following to use illustrative material is gratefully acknowledged: Bingham Library, Cirencester; Corinium Museum, Cirencester; Cirencester Excavation Committee; Miss J. Stacey, Headmistress, Cirencester County Infants' School, and Mr. J. Edmonds, Headmaster, Cirencester County Junior School.

'Corinium' and 'Cirencester'

It is thought that the Roman name 'Corinium' may have been associated with the British word Corn or Cor(i)n which also appears in the name of the British tribe, the Cornovii, whose territory was based in the Shropshire area. It is even possible that the Dobunni may have been a branch of the Cornovii. The same word is found in the River Churn and Cerney.

The Anglo-Saxons added 'cester' (derived from Latin, castra = camp) to the first part of the Roman name, although the change from 'Corin' to 'Ciren' is not easily explained. The earliest Anglo-Saxon form known is Cirenceaster, pronounced, it is assumed, with a hard 'c'. Norman French influence softened the 'c' sound to the present pronunciation.

Various forms appear from medieval times such as Cyrencestre (1156), Cisetur (1453) and Sisator (1685).

Preface

It is impossible to do justice to Cirencester's complex and colourful history in one short volume. This is an attempt to present in a continuous and coherent form, the story of the town's development from Roman times to the present day, set against the background of the national events which influenced it. The conclusions of much recent archaeological and historical research have been incorporated in the text and it is hoped that the book will prove useful and interesting both to general readers and to students as a basis for further study. Suggestions for places to visit appear at the end of each chapter.

I am deeply grateful to the many people who have helped and encouraged me in this task – in particular Linda and David Viner who have given generously of their time and expertise; Joyce Barker who read the manuscript and made invaluable comments and suggestions; the staffs of the County Record Office, Gloucester City Library and Bingham Library, Cirencester for their unfailing helpfulness and courtesy and above all my husband, Alan, without whom the whole enterprise would have been unthinkable.

Roman Cirencester

Most of Roman Cirencester lies under the buildings of successive generations of later citizens. Only the work of today's archaeologists, following the efforts of earlier less well-equipped enthusiasts, makes inhabitants and visitors increasingly aware of the wealth and complexity of the second largest city in Roman Britain which is beneath their feet.

In pre-Roman times the site of the later town was apparently unimportant. Although recent archaeological evidence indicates the presence of Iron Age farms on the well-drained alluvial soil of the river Churn, the centres of tribal power and trade lay in the heavily defended hill-forts. By late in the first century A.D. Gloucestershire east of the Severn Vale formed part of the kingdom of the Dobunni. The excavations at Bagendon, 4.8km. north of Cirencester in 1962 by Mrs E.M. Clifford, revealed an extensive settlement or oppidum which might have been the Dobunnic tribal capital at this time. Coin moulds found here suggested that this was also the site of the official mint, normally situated in the main settlement. The Dobunni, from the evidence of other finds at Bagendon, were farmers, living on this 200 acre (81 hectares) site in timber-framed huts with enclosures for their stock. They were also skilful metal workers, using Mendip lead and Forest of Dean iron as well as tin, copper and gold from further afield. They imported pottery from Gaul and glass from the Levant.

From the evidence of their coins, it seems likely that by the time the Roman legions landed in Kent in A.D. 43, the Dobunni were divided into two groups – one under King Boduocus or Bodvoc, probably living at Bagendon or Corinion as it might have been known, the other half ruled by a king whose full name is uncertain but which began with Corio ... This part of the Dobunni could have been based at Minchinhampton where extensive earthworks have been found. One authority, Professor John Wacher, has suggested that by the time of the Roman

1

invasion, the Dobunni under Boduocus had been conquered by the most powerful British tribe in the south-east, the Catuvellauni, and that Boduocus was merely a puppet ruler. Whatever the relationship between the tribes, however, it seems probable that the Dobunni were among those who submitted to the Emperor Claudius in August A.D. 43.

Within the next few years the land of the Dobunni was occupied, with little resistance in the Cirencester area. The Romans followed their customary pattern of maintaining control by building roads and inter-linked forts as they pushed forward, enabling supplies and troops to be moved speedily and protecting their rear.

It is thought that there was a fort at Cirencester in the first years of the Roman occupation. The site was a natural choice – it was an important crossing of the River Churn and, being on a low plateau with rising ground to the south and west, was easily defensible. It would also be easy from here to keep a watchful eye on the Dobunnic capital at Bagendon, if necessary. The precise date of the construction of the major routes of the Fosse Way, its branch Akeman Street, and Ermin Street is not easy to establish but the convergence of these at Cirencester also made it an important road junction. A section of Ermin Street linked Cirencester with Gloucester and the fort at Kingsholm, while the Fosse Way provided communication from Lincoln to Exeter. Ancient trackways, such as the Whiteway, were also utilised.

The early fort was probably dismantled after the initial period of conquest and recent archaeological opinion dates the first significant military installation at Cirencester to A.D. 49. The evidence for this later fort was found in 1961 on the Leaholme site, lying between The Avenue and the gardens of Watermoor House, covering an area of 1.8 hectares (4.5 acres), just large enough for a cavalry unit or alae of 500 men. The Romans maintained a miltary presence in Cirencester until the early or middle 70's A.D. Changes in the garrison were likely over a period of some 20 years and the tombstones of two Roman soldiers found in the nineteenth century in the Watermoor area show that at least two cavalry regiments were stationed here. One of the soldiers, Dannicus, was a trooper of the cavalry regiment Indiana, originally from Switzerland; the other, Sextus Valerius Genialis, was from the Low Countries. The Roman army recruited its forces from all parts of the Empire and these men, like many others, had marched far from their homelands in its

Tombstone erected to Dannicus, a cavalryman, found in the Watermoor area.
Courtesy Corinium Museum.

service. Changes in the fort itself as well as its personnel were indicated by excavations on The Sands site (Chesterton Lane) and in the grounds of Watermoor Hospital, now the offices of the Cotswold District Council. Structures revealed here could have been a part of a large annexe to the Leaholme fort.

As the Romans pushed westwards there was no longer the need for a permanent garrison at Cirencester. The fort was dismantled and the cavalry pulled out, leaving behind some of their belongings, including a pile of Samian ware which appeared never to have been issued from the quarter-master's stores. By this time a civilian settlement of wooden huts had grown up to the north-west of the fort. The Dobunnic traders, no doubt attracted by the ready market which this offered, had been leaving their capital at Bagendon. The Bagendon excavations showed that the number of people living there declined between A.D. 43 and A.D. 60. This new settlement probably had the status of a village or vicus, managing its affairs under Roman supervision. When the Roman military authority left this was the obvious basis for the civil administration. The existing tribe, the Dobunni, now became the local authority or civitas with an elected council and officials and a capital – Corinium Dobunnorum.

The land on which the fort had stood was presumably handed over to the new civil authority for it was here that the centre of the town of Corinium began to be constructed. Like any other Roman town the most important buildings were the basilica and the forum. Work on the basilica began in the last quarter of the first century A.D. First located and identified by Wilfred Cripps in 1897–8, the site of this is partially marked out in the area off The Avenue bounded by the Masonic Hall and the entrance to St. Michael's Field. Its asymmetrical plan was unusual and its size, 100 metres long and 24 metres wide, made it, with the adjacent forum, larger than any comparable complex in Roman Britain except London. It was constructed of limestone, perhaps brought from the Querns, and divided into a nave and two aisles. It was richly decorated with mouldings of Purbeck marble and Italian marble veneers. On its south-east side was a range of rooms and somewhere within it would have been a shrine possibly to a local deity. Despite the obvious wealth expended on the building, the site was not entirely suitable – by the middle of the second century A.D. the basilica began to sink into the ditches of the fort over which it had been built and major repairs had to be

4

Socket with eagle's head, a cart fitting found in Querns Lane.
Courtesy Corinium Museum.

carried out.

It was from the basilica that the local administration of the community was organised, for it was Rome's policy to shift such burdens as tax collection and public works on to the native population. Here also, in the basilica, the elected decurions would have dealt with petty crime or civil disputes, imposing fines or confiscation of property on the guilty. Imprisonment was not a usual punishment and there seem to have been no gaols in Roman Britain. On the north-west side of the basilica the inhabitants of Corinium would have congregated in the forum, either to chat with friends and acquaintances in the vast paved courtyard (108 metres by 68 metres) or to visit the shops and offices reached by the covered colonnade which surrounded three sides of the courtyard. They would have met also in the public baths but these remain yet to be discovered, as do the mansio or inn where tired travellers would have found accommodation and fresh horses.

The streets of Corinium were planned in the fashion of most Roman towns, laid out at right angles to each other, forming rectangular blocks of land or insulae, averaging 158 metres by

Detail from the Four Seasons mosaic showing Acteon transformed into a stag and attacked by his own dogs. *Courtesy Corinium Museum.*

100 metres. The exact location of many of these streets has not been established but the re-constructed plan of Corinium shows the line of Ermin Street, entering the town by the Silchester gate, located in the Watermoor Road area, crossing the Fosse Way near the present junction of Lewis Lane and Tower Street at South Way, and leaving through another gate, probably under the hump at the junction of Gloucester Street and Spitalgate Lane. The Fosse Way, merging with Akeman Street in the London Road, enters Corinium through the north-east or 'Verulamium' gate, follows the line of Lewis Lane and Querns Lane to the Bath Gate, the site of which is marked in Phoenix Way. Like its modern successor, Corinium was the meeting point of important major highways.

In the early years of its existence Corinium had no defences and it was not until the second century A.D. that the town was surrounded by an earth rampart with stone towers at intervals. The town gates probably first date from the same period. The river Churn was diverted into the ditches on the eastern side of the town and a bridge built outside the north-east gate. This gate was excavated in 1960 and although only a part was found, it was deduced that it had four portals with two central carriage-ways, each 4 metres wide, flanked by two subsidiary paths of 3.1 metres each. On either side of the gate were projecting towers. The volume of vehicular traffic had been great enough to cause deep ruts in the road surface. The Bath Gate, excavated in 1974, was smaller, with two portals only, though of the same design. Repairs to the gates were obviously necessary over the years. At the beginning of the fourth century, for example, it was found that the north-east gate and its adjoining wall had been damaged by flooding. To deal with the problem a sluice gate was cut through the wall close to the gateway to lessen the water pressure against the stonework. The town's defences were also improved in later years. In the first half of the third century the existing earth bank was faced with a thick stone wall, varying in width from 1.2 to 3 metres and about one hundred years later some external bastions were added.

The Roman defences left a mark on the landscape which is still visible in the form of a grass bank beside the river in the Abbey Grounds, along Beeches Road to the City Bank Playing Field and in the grounds of Watermoor School. The only length of the wall permanently exposed is that in the Abbey Grounds, restored 1967–72. Doubtless over the centuries the walls provided useful material for builders although much must have remained stand-ing for a long period. In 1540 John Leland reported seeing 'the cumpace of fundacion of towers sumtyme standing in the waul' and Rudder, writing at the end of the eighteenth century noted that on a visit in 1723, Dr Stukeley 'fancied that he could even trace the old city walls right round the town'.

The area of the city which these walls enclosed was about 96 hectares, making Corinium second in size only to London in Roman Britain, although there were parts, like the lower lying marshy district, which were never built on.

By the early years of the second century a new market hall, probably for butchers, had been erected on ground next to the forum. Animal remains from this area are largely of ox, sheep and pig, and suggest that they may have been slaughtered and butchered nearby. Gnawed bones indicate the presence of dogs on the site. Meat pies were possibly baked near the meat market – ovens and other items of baking equipment have been disco-

Reconstruction of a Roman kitchen and hypocaust system, Corinum Museum.
Courtesy Corinium Museum.

vered in a row of shops across the street.

Corinium must have offered excellent shopping facilities to its inhabitants. Provisions ranged from local produce and freshly baked bread to wine and oil imported from the Mediterranean. Pottery and glassware from Gaul and beyond were available as well as articles produced in Corinium's own workshops. A crucible, containing gold specks, found in the market hall might have belonged to a goldsmith. Evidence of bone working indicates the production of bone pins and needles. The name of at least one sculptor working in Cirencester, Sulinus, is known and the sculptures displayed in the Corinium Museum are convincing proof of the fine quality of the craftsmanship of the period.

In a large urban centre such as Corinium it is also likely that people would have found advice on the treatment of physical ailments. There is not much direct evidence of any doctor working here but at least two eye specialists are known to have practised in the town. Their instructions for the use of their remedies have survived – cut into stone stamps which were then impressed into the solid form of the prescription, ready for it to be liquified by the user:–

'Atticus' frankincense salve
For all pains to be made up with egg'

Most of the shops and workshops were probably located in the

8

Reconstruction of a Roman triclinium, Corinium Museum, showing the Four
Seasons mosaic.   *Courtesy Corinium Museum.*

area around the forum or fronting the main thoroughfare on
Ermin Street. By the second century, like many domestic buildings, they would have been built of stone, with roofs of ceramic
or stone tiles. Some shops were only lock-ups; others would
have had living quarters behind their narrow street frontage. The
streets were made of packed gravel or limestone rubble, and,
when necessary a layer of similar material was simply thrown
onto the surface, thus causing levels to rise by as much as 3
metres in the 350 or so years of the town's existence. In wet
weather the dusty, powdery surface of the streets was turned to
mud and although at first the internal floor level of shops and
houses could be raised to prevent mud washing through the front
door, eventually the occupant would have little choice but to
rebuild his property completely.

Archaeological evidence illustrates the wealth and sophistica-
tion of some of Corinium's inhabitants who adopted the Roman
way of life. The walls of their houses were plastered and
decorated in bright colours, they enjoyed the benefit of central

Winged Sea Serpent and Dolphin from the Hunting Dogs mosaic found in Dyer Street and now in Corinium Museum.   *Courtesy Corinium Museum.*

heating through the hypocaust system, and they had private bath suites. Their tables were graced by the finest Samian ware and their rooms were embellished with lamps and statues. Above all, this opulence is epitomised in the magnificent mosaic pavements, about eighty of which have been recorded. Some date from the second century – such as those of the Hunting Dogs and the Seasons, discovered in Dyer Street in 1849. However, it was in the fourth century that the craft of the mosaicist reached its peak and the most elaborate floors were laid. The similarities in these pavements have led authorities to believe that many were the work of a particular firm, based in Corinium – hence their attributing to the so-called 'Corinian School'. One of its most popular designs depicts Orpheus surrounded by birds and animals. Such pavements were found in Dyer Street and at Barton Farm.

Another of the amenities of the thriving town was the amphitheatre which lies about 270 metres to the south-west outside the town wall. The seating banks, on which the citizens of Corinium once congregated to watch bear-baiting or wrestling at the expense of local magistrates at election times or during religious festivals, are now grass-covered mounds up to 8 metres high. It seems that there were at least thirty rows of seats which could have accommodated between 6,000–8,000 people – perhaps an indication of the town's potential population. It is likely that a town such as Corinium would also have had a theatre. Curving walls, found near the probable site of the Gloucester gate, suggest that it might have been located in this area.

No temples have as yet been identified in Corinium although there must have been several, as well as a number of smaller shrines. The Roman authorities were tolerant of a wide range of religious practices. Visiting traders and officials would have had favourite deities while the Dobunni had their own special cults such as the Genii Cucullati, mysterious hooded figures representing godlets of fertility, healing and the other world. Sometimes these are accompanied by a Mother Goddess. A representation of the Deae Matres, the three mother goddesses, was found when Ashcroft Road was being constructed and can be seen in the Corinium Museum. The cult of Jupiter was also popular and columns dedicated to him appear to have been set up in the town. The capital of such a column with fine statuary was found in 1838 and is also displayed in the Corinium Museum.

In A.D. 312 the Emperor Constantine decreed Christianity the official religion of the Empire and two years later in A.D 314 four British Bishops, one of whom may have come from Corinium attended the Church Council at Arles. If there was a representative from Corinium there must by this time have been a Christian community in the town although no archaeological evidence for this at present exists apart from the famous word square found in Victoria Road in 1868. Scratched on a piece of wall plaster this resembles examples found elsewhere in the Roman world and is considered a possible Christian symbol. Translated literally a rather meaningless phrase emerges but if the letters are re-arranged to form a cross, a message of Christian significance appears. As such concealment would not have been necessary by the early years of the fourth century, it could be taken as proof of Christian worship in the earlier period of the Roman occupation.

All the popular religious cults laid stress on the importance of the proper burial of the body. The law required that all bodies had to be buried outside the town limits. Cemeteries have been

Sculpture of the Deae Matres found in Ashcroft, now in Corinium Museum.
Courtesy Corinium Museum.

Capital from a Corinthian column dedicated to Jupiter.

Courtesy Corinium Museum.

The word square found in Victoria Road in 1868. Literally the message reads 'The Sower Arepo holds the wheel carefully'. The letters can be re-arranged to form PATERNOSTER down and across, leaving A and O (twice) which can be interpreted as Alpha and Omega – the beginning and the end.

Courtesy Corinium Museum.

located outside all the major gates of Corinium. Excavations outside the Bath Gate between 1969 and 1978 produced 453 burials. Dr. Alan McWhirr has pointed out that if the population of the town was in the region of 5–10,000, assuming an average life span of forty years, in 400 years, 50–100,000 dead would be produced. Therefore, 453 burials represents less than one per cent of the population during the Roman occupation. Nevertheless the information gained from the study of the skeletons is invaluable. Three of the burials were cremations, the rest inhumations. Many seem to have been buried in wooden coffins, wearing their shoes. There were two and a half times more females than males, a puzzling fact for which there appears no reasonable explanation. The average male height was 5 ft 6.5 inches, for women 5 ft 2 inches. The good condition of their teeth suggests that they had enjoyed a reasonable diet with adequate supplies of meat and not excessive carbohydrates. The evidence of bone fractures pointed to a vigorous active life which had involved many accidents. Some of the fractures had healed badly indicating perhaps a lack of professional attention. The commonest identifiable disease was osteo-arthritis. Although it was the Roman custom to furnish graves with objects to aid the passage into the next world, very few items for this purpose were found. A child of three had the richest burial – in a wooden coffin with a silver clasped bead necklace and bone bracelets on each wrist. In two burials adults had coins placed in the mouth – the traditional payment for the ferryman, Charon, to row them across the River Styx to Hades.

Many burials will have been destroyed by the activities of later generations. The tombstones of the cavalrymen already referred to indicate the existence of a miltary cemetery in the Watermoor area. Here also was found the earliest recorded civilian tombstone, Philus from Gaul, probably a trader following the army. The antiquarian Dr. Stukeley, visiting the town in 1723, reported seeing an inscription to Julia Casta aged 33, which had been found 'at a place half a mile west of the town upon the north side of the Foss Road called the Querns'.

In the early years of the fourth century, Britain was divided into four provinces and it is probable that Corinium became the capital of one of these – Britannia Prima. A stone found near Victoria Road in 1891, part of a column dedicated to Jupiter bears the inscription 'Lucius Septimius, Governor of Britannia Prima restored (this monument)'.

Members of the Ermin Street Guard examining the Hare mosaic found at the Beeches. *Courtesy Corinium Museum.*

At this period changes were made to the town centre which might have been connected with the setting up of the provincial government. The basilica was remodelled – the rooms on the south-east side now faced towards the street instead of towards the hall and this street was shut off at one end by a row of shops. The effect was to enclose a new area. The forum too was divided by a wall running across its central courtyard. On its north-west wing part of the colonnade was enclosed and a mosaic floor laid. Perhaps the northern part of the forum was given over to the business of the provinical governor and this new enclosed area of the basilica was a recompense to the trading community for the loss of market space.

During the later fourth century some of the hitherto undeveloped areas of the town were built on. In 1970–73 excavations took place on the Beeches Road allotments' site, just inside the Town Wall. Two or possibly three houses were found, containing tessellated pavements including that of the fine hare mosaic. One of these houses was similar in plan to the winged corridor villa

16

more usually the centre of a farm and the finding of an iron coulter from a Roman plough and four bone plaques used in weaving have led experts to postulate that this group of buildings was connected with agriculture and that there was a community of farmers in this part of the town, possibly with their own smithies.

The implication of this theory is that in the early fourth century, if not before, the land immediately around the town was being worked from inside its walls. This and the suggestion that the settlement at the Barton also included a farm has renewed the discussion of the relationship of Corinium to the surrounding countryside. Until late in the third century most of the land in Gloucestershire was worked by the indigenous population in the traditional pre-Roman fashion. The neighbouring farmers presumably would have availed themselves of the facilities offered by the market at Corinium. The original buildings at Chedworth are earlier than the majority of the great villa-estates of Gloucestershire which date from late third or early fourth century, so it is probable that some of the produce from Chedworth, some nine kilometres from Corinium also reached the latter's market, over a considerable period of time.

The early years of the fourth century under the Emperor Constantine saw the height of Britain's prosperity but this was shortlived. When he died in A.D. 337, the Empire was divided among his three sons and before long conflict ensued between them. To add to the internal problems, the frontiers of the Empire were assaulted by barbarian raids. A contemporary historian Ammianus reflected the general apprehension when in 360 he wrote of the 'pall of fear which lay over the provinces'. In Britain such fear was increased by the concerted barbarian attacks in 367 – in the south and east by the Saxons and the Franks, by the Picts who poured over Hadrian's Wall and the Scots who sailed acoss the Irish Sea to land in the north. Under the Emperor Theodosius (A.D. 379–395) Britain's defences were strengthened and at least a semblance of order restored but the great days of Roman authority were over. The effects of such events particularly on the inland towns is of course conjectural but the inhabitants of Corinium like others must have felt the general uncertainty and even at times panic as news reached them. Indeed one authority, Dr. Richard Reece, has suggested that the towns were already unrecognisable as such by as early as A.D. 350. Whatever view is taken of the state of affairs in Britain during the last years of Roman rule, it is quite clear that the golden age of Corinium, second city of Roman Britain, had ended.

WHAT TO SEE

● Restored portion of Roman wall in Abbey Grounds. The line of the eastern defences can be followed from the earth bank alongside the river in the Abbey Grounds to Beeches Road and the City Bank Playing Field in Watermoor.

● The amphitheatre – entrance in Cotswold Avenue, off Querns Hill.

● The sites of the south-west end of the basilica, off The Avenue, the crossing of two major Roman roads near the modern junction of Lewis Lane and South Way, Bath Gate in Phoenix Way and the Verulamium Gate in the London Road are marked by plaques erected by Cirencester Civic Society.

● For a complete tour of Roman remains which survive above ground see Viner, D., The Corinium Trail, A Guide to Roman Cirencester (Corinium Museum Publications).

● Finds from the Bagendon site and an extensive collection of Roman antiquities including material from recent excavations are on display in the Corinium Museum, Park Street.

Saxons, Danes and Normans

'And never since have the Romans reigned in Britain'. Thus the end of Roman rule is recorded by the Anglo-Saxon Chronicle as occurring in A.D. 435. The Chronicle was probably written in the ninth century and its early chronology is suspect but it is established from other sources that by A.D. 410 the regular Roman army had been withdrawn from Britain leaving the inhabitants to cope with both military and civil affairs. Archaeological evidence suggests that at least for the first years of the fifth century there were attempts in Corinium to maintain the pattern of life of the previous 350 or so years. The town's defences were being repaired and the floor of the forum cleaned, even when its paving stones were very worn so that if it was no longer fully operational as a market and commercial centre, there was sufficient civic pride and organisation to create a semblance of order. Few coins were found, indicating that the forum was being swept at least until these had ceased to circulate – a date estimated by one authority, Dr. J.P.C. Kent, at A.D. 430.

At some point after this the civic authority disintegrated. A ditch beside Ermin Street was found to contain leaves and grass rather than the silt from the road surface, formed by traffic. Two bodies discovered in the same ditch, a little distance away, had not been properly buried. The town appears to have been virtually abandoned. It has been postulated that there could have been an outbreak of plague. Such outbreaks did occur in western provinces of the Empire in the fifth and sixth centuries and Bede, writing in the eighth century speaks of a terrible plague at this period which 'in a short while destroyed so large a number that the living could scarcely bury the dead'. Whatever happened to the once flourishing city of Corinium there is at present no evidence that it met a violent end.

By the mid-fifth century the Germanic mercenaries and their families brought in by the Romans to bolster Britain's defences against the barbarian raids, had been joined by further waves of

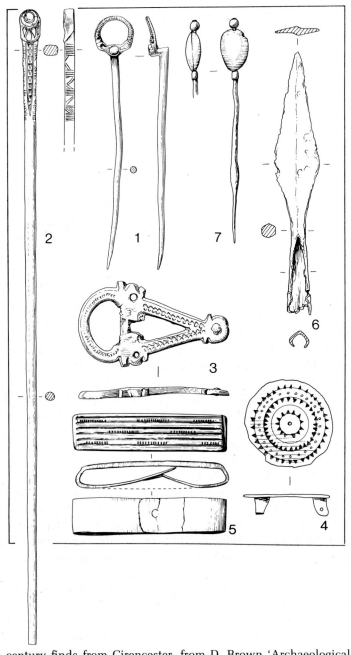

5th–6th century finds from Cirencester, from D. Brown 'Archaeological Evidence for the Anglo-Saxon Period'. *BAR. Vol. 30* (Scale 1–5, 7:$\frac{2}{3}$; 6: $\frac{1}{3}$).

Germanic settlers. Some of these had perhaps been invited by the Britons themselves, others came on their own initiative, seeking new land. As the newcomers infiltrated into the Thames valley area it seems that for sometime there was peaceful co-existence between them and the settled population. The Anglo-Saxon cemetery at the Barton, best known for the graves of two Saxon warriors found, in 1909, to have been cut through the Orpheus pavement, is thought to have been in use in the first half of the sixth century. If this view is accepted, there would presumably have been an established Saxon community in the vicinity before the famous battle of 577 recorded by the Anglo-Saxon Chronicle. 'This year Cuthwin and Ceawlin fought with the Britons and slew three Kings, Conmail, and Condidan and Farinmail on the spot that is called Derham (Dyrham) and took from them three cities, Gloucester, Cirencester and Bath'. This may have been the last stand of organised British resistance in the area against a more aggressive Saxon thrust from the west. Perhaps it was here that the Saxon warrior, one of those mentioned above, whose bones now lie peacefully in the Corinium Museum, met his death. Was the city mentioned as Cirencester, the remnant of the old Roman town or had the British population of the area established themselves elsewhere? Excavations at the amphitheatre in 1962 showed that it was being used well on in the fifth century and that its original construction had been altered. In other parts of the Roman Empire amphitheatres were fortified against attack. It is possible that this happened at Cirencester and that it was the amphitheatre which was over-run in 577.

The history of Cirencester from this date until the Norman Conquest has to be pieced together from fragmentary archaeological and documentary evidence and much perforce has to be conjectural. The miscellaneous finds such as pins, buckles, beads and garter hooks dating from fifth to tenth century are insufficient to establish the nature of the settlement which, taking into consideration the medieval town plan, appears to have been growing up on the drier ground north-west of the Roman city in the modern Cecily Hill area. From what we know of such settlements the inhabitants would have lived in one-roomed timber-framed huts, with walls of wattle and daub and thatched roofs, a far cry from the Roman town houses now deserted and in ruins only a little distance away.

After 577 there is no further mention of Cirencester in the

21

Part of the Roman amphitheatre, today.   *Photo. A. Welsford.*

Anglo-Saxon Chronicle for another fifty years or so when in 628
Cynegils of Wessex was defeated here by Penda, King of Mercia
From this date, except for the brief reign of Edgar (829–30),
Cirencester was under Mercian domination, forming part of the
territory of the Hwicce. The kingdom of the Hwicce was one of
the many small kingdoms within Mercia and their territory
included Gloucestershire east of the Severn, Worcestershire and
the western half of Warwickshire. By the early eighth century
Mercia was the leading power south of the Humber and Offa
(757–96) the most powerful English king before Alfred. Cirencester, though, lying near the border with Wessex, was probably
considered too vulnerable for a royal seat and it was Winchcombe, sixteen miles to the north, which was thus favoured.

Towards the end of the ninth century, however, the rivalries of
Mercia and Wessex were submerged by the greater threat from
the Danes. By 870 their activities had brought to an end the
kingdoms of Northumbria and East Anglia and their army was
encamped at Reading poised for the attack on Wessex. Initially
defeated, they renewed the fight in the following year. Alfred,
now King of Wessex, bought off the Danes for the next five years
during which period they expelled King Burgred of Mercia and

22

replaced him with their own nominee. It seems likely that at this time there would have been Danes in Cirencester itself, though their impact on the existing population is unknown. It has been pointed out that Inchthorpe (medieval Instrop), which is an old name for Cecily Hill, is one of the nineteen examples of Gloucestershire place names ending in 'thorpe' meaning 'village' which can be either Scandinavian or Saxon in origin. Two other local names with the same ending are Hatherop and Southrop.

The decisive defeat of the Danes at Ethandune (Edington) in 878 prevented any further Danish expansion westward. At the Treaty of Wedmore they agreed to withdraw behind a line stretching roughly from London to Chester and to accept the Christian faith. Guthrum, the Danish leader then came to Cirencester where, the Anglo-Saxon Chronicle records, the Danes 'remained a whole year before moving into East Anglia'. It is something of a mystery why the Danes should have stayed in Cirencester. Perhaps here, just over the border from Wessex and commanding a good road position, it would have been possible to maintain some supervision over them and to superintend their religious instruction although we have no evidence how, if at all, these tasks were undertaken.

After the Danish withdrawal into East Anglia, occasional references suggest that at some time before the Norman Conquest, Cirencester became a royal manor or 'tun' where the king occasionally held his council. In 999 Ethelred the Unready issued a charter from here ordering the banishment of Earl Aelfric who had appropriated land from a widow, Eathflaed of South Cerney. In 1020 the Anglo-Saxon Chronicle mentions a great Council at Cirencester held by King Cnut at Easter. It could be implied from such information that Cirencester had become the focus of the administration of the surrounding district.

Whether Christianity survived in Cirencester in the immediate post-Roman period is debatable. A Roman origin has sometimes been attributed to the medieval chapel of St. Cecilia which, until the late fifteenth century is believed to have stood on the south side of Cecily Hill. St. Cecilia was a popular saint in Roman Britain. However, the chapel might have been an early Norman foundation, linked with William I's daughter, Cecilia, Abbess of Caen, rather than a Roman establishment continuing into the Anglo-Saxon period. Bede states that by the 680's the Hwicce had become Christian and that the Archbishop of Canterbury, Theodore of Tarsus, created the diocese of Worcester for them

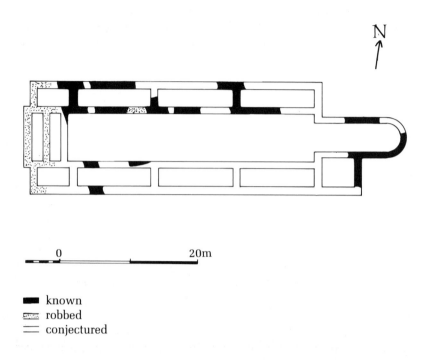

N ↑

0   20m

■ known
▦ robbed
═ conjectured

A plan of the Saxon church at Cirencester, excavated in 1965. After D. Brown in McWhirr (ed.) 1976.

(Gloucestershire, east of the Severn, remained in the diocese of Worcester until the Reformation).

Archaeological evidence of the Anglo-Saxon church in Cirencester derives from excavations on the Abbey site in 1965 and 1966. A large pre-Conquest church and crypt had been built here at some time from the late seventh to the ninth centuries in the opinion of the Director of the excavation, David Brown. The foundations of the church were of re-used Roman material, either taken from the site itself or possibly from Roman buildings still standing. Before the Norman Conquest, in the current view, this large church had been demolished and replaced by a smaller building. If this had actually happened several possible reasons have been suggested. If the first church had been built before the ninth century it might have been a target for Danish raiders, known to be in the Severn valley area (893–5). If it had not been built until early in the tenth century it might still have been subject to Danish attentions since as late as 1015 Cnut's army crossed the Thames at Cricklade, marched through Gloucestershire to Warwickshire and 'ravaged and burnt and killed all they came across' (Anglo-Saxon Chronicle). Developments in English parochial organisation from the tenth century onwards might also account for the original church being replaced by a smaller structure. The parochiae of the tenth century were sometimes later subdivided – hence the number of village churches, often built by local landowners which show early eleventh century features – two such, close to Cirencester, are Daglingworth and Duntisbourne Rous. A large church at Cirencester intended to serve a wide area, might also be considered too large for its diminishing responsibilities and could have been replaced even if its predecessor had not been damaged by the Danes.

In the late Anglo-Saxon period local civil organisation was also being formalised. The system was based on the administrative and legal units of the hundred and the shire. Theoretically the hundred consisted of 100 hides (a hide = 120 acres) but the number of hides in a hundred seems to have varied. The hide, perhaps more significantly, had become a fixed unit of taxation, providing English kings with a highly sophisticated and efficient method of tax assessment. Assessments for taxation and for a community's military commitments were made at the hundred court. Each hundred was divided into tithings, groups of ten households, mutually responsible for lawkeeping. These arrangements also formed the basis of the later medieval administration and are reflected in Cirencester in the districts or tithings of Chesterton, Spiringate and Barton.

In the medieval period Cirencester itself was the centre of a hundred with its own court. It may be, as one authority (T.R. Slater) has suggested, that, as a royal manor in Saxon times, Cirencester might have held a similar position then. Nevertheless it was Gloucester and not Cirencester which gave its name to the shire whose legal, administrative and military functions were superior to those of the hundred.

This existing Anglo-Saxon organisation was utilised by their Norman conquerors as a basis for the great Domesday survey conducted twenty years after William, Duke of Normandy had defeated Harold at Hastings. The object of the survey, initiated by William at his Christmas court in Gloucester in 1085 was of course to give the king and his ministers a clear estimate of the taxable value of each district and who was in occupation. The details of contemporary society gleaned by later generations are coincidental to its original purpose. For the bulk of the population in Gloucestershire the Conquest probably meant little change. The survey does not suggest any widespread economic depression of the peasantry. Many of the characteristics of later manorial organisation can be discerned in the pre-Conquest period. A change of master probably meant that some of the customary duties were more strictly enforced. However, for the old English nobility and smaller landed gentry in Gloucestershire, the changes were catastrophic – not one of their names is amongst the secular tenants-in-chief and in Cirencester as in many other areas, lesser tenants were also ousted.

Information for the survey was gathered by the King's commissioners at the shire courts to which the present tenants and representatives of each hundred were summoned. We can imagine the men from Cirencester testifying to the correctness of their answers to the lengthy number of questions:– about the current ownership of land, its present extent and value and what it was worth and who owned it at the time of Edward the Confessor, how many men worked the land, how much meadow and woodland there was, how many mills and so on. The completed entries in the survey give many details about this early Norman community in Cirencester. At the Conquest in 1066, the royal manor of Cirencester comprised five hides together with the manor of Minety. It had meadows and woods worth five shillings. One of the woods was that of Achelie (or Oakley), the other was in the parish of Minety and was part of the ancient royal forest of Cemele or Bradon. Three mills were recorded valued at thirty shillings, presumably the two mentioned in later documents at Barton and that near the 'Gilden Bridge' over the Churn (at the end of Gloucester Street). Before 1066 the manor had paid rent both in money and kind – annually £9 5s, grain, honey and 3,000 loaves for the royal hunting dogs. It had obviously been well managed in the years after the Conquest – its rent had risen to £20 5s, and 20 pigs and 20 cows had been substituted for the grain and honey. The 3,000 loaves for the dogs had been commuted to a payment of 16s! In the days of Edward the Confessor the Queen had received the wool from the sheep – a significant reference considering the future importance of wool to the town. It is the only reference to wool in the whole of the Gloucestershire survey although there must have been other sheep kept in the district since the Domesday entry for Kempsford records that the sheepfold there produced 120 lbs. of cheese.

William I granted the manor of Cirencester to William Fitz Osbern whom he created Earl of Hereford. William Fitz Osbern's son Roger inherited it on his father's death but after his rebellion in 1075 it again reverted to the Crown. According to the Domesday record the lord of the manor of Cirencester had five ploughs, there were thirty-one villagers with ten ploughs and ten smallholders. The arable land of the manor would have been in two or three large open field unenclosed by hedges. The thirty-one villagers would have used their ploughs on a co-operative basis for few peasants were rich enough to own the eight oxen needed for each plough. Each would have had the tenancy of land in these fields – probably about thirty acres in return for specific duties. Some might have had to work regularly each week on the lord's land, others might be expected to weed his crops or carry his produce to market. At harvest time all were required. The lord's own demesne land might be part of the main fields or separate. It is thought that the Barton Grange farm of the medieval Cirencester abbey could have been the site of the earlier manor demesne farm. The ten smallholders were less well off than the villagers or villeins. They did service for a tenancy of about five acres and probably also paid a monthly rent. There were also thirteen serfs who had no land at all and were virtually at the beck and call of their lord. In quite a different category were the two freemen each with a plough who have been identified as the holders of the two sub-manors with houses in what later became Dyer Street. The manor of Archebaldes lay on the south side and initally the family held their land by virtue of keeping the king's greyhounds. Presumably this custom later lapsed since in the reign of Henry III (1216–1272) a descendant was fined for failing to do so. On the north side was the manor of de Pyrie. The de Pyrie land was gradually alienated to the abbey in the medieval period but most of the Archebaldes' estate survived intact until the sixteenth century.

Other parts of the original Saxon manor had been detached before the Domesday survey. William Fitz Osbern had granted two hides to an unknown freeman and this land has been identified as the medieval manor of Wiggold which lay east of Baunton. The two hide manor of Chesterton had presumably been separated at an earlier date. It was held at Domesday by William de Baderon. At the time of the Conquest it had been in the possession of a Saxon, Alfwy, an example of a Norman replacing an English occupant. The mill belonging to Chesterton manor was in the Watermoor area, later known at Langley's mill after the lords of this manor from thirteenth to sixteenth centuries. The sixteenth century mill buildings survive as two cottages on City Bank.

The first mention of a market at Cirencester comes from this period when the Domesday entry states that the annual tolls raised were 20 shillings. Presumably since the market is referred to as 'new' it had either not long been in existence or it had replaced an earlier one. The market would have served the immediate south Cotswold area as the upper Thames valley, south of Cirencester, would have looked more naturally to Cricklade.

The church was entitled to a third of the market tolls. From the time of Edward the Confessor the church had also held two hides free of any dues with six acres of meadow. The total value of this was 40 shillings. William I had added woodland at Painswick, valued at 10 shillings. The claim that, in 1066, there was a college of secular canons at the church has recently been challenged by Dr. Babette Evans. This claim had been based on the testimony of John Collinson, the eighteenth century historian of Somerset and one time curate at Cirencester, that he had seen a manuscript (of which there is now no trace) which showed that a collegiate church had been founded in Cirencester in the ninth century in the reign of Egbert. The Domesday entry gives no indication as to whether there were one or more priests here in 1086. A two hide endowment, although generous for a parish church, is not considered to have been sufficient to support more than two or three priests at most and then only very modestly. There certainly were canons at Cirencester when the Abbey was founded by Henry I in 1117 since the abbey's charter makes specific reference to them. It is possible that these could have arrived or their numbers have been increased in the thirty-one years between the Domesday survey and the foundation of the abbey.

Controversy also surrounds the figure of Regenbald who until recently was accepted as Dean of this college of canons and also Chancellor to Edward the Confessor. That he held either of these offices has been questioned by Dr. Evans. Deans are said not to have been introduced into English churches until after the Norman Conquest and although it is known from contemporary

28

Excavations on the Abbey site. Nave foundations of the Abbey church looking West: Saxon foundations in the centre; 12th century foundations on the left, with Roman walls diagonally aligned.

Courtesy Cirencester Excavations Committee.

sources that Regenbald served both the Confessor and the Conqueror as one of a clerical staff of priests there is no evidence that he had any special position under Edward – indeed there was then no such recognisable office. It is just possible that he was Chancellor to William I for a very brief period at the beginning of his reign but more probably the title was a retrospective embellishment by someone associated with the abbey of which Regenbald was considered a benefactor.

There is no doubt, however, that Regenbald had connections with Cirencester – in one charter he is referred to as 'Regenbald of Cirencester' – and that he enjoyed royal patronage. He had acquired partly from Edward the Confessor, partly from William

I, an estate of some ninety hides, worth at least £40 a year. Edward the Confessor also granted him the legal status of a bishop since presumably he could not take a bishopric either because of marriage or unchastity. His connection with the Cirencester area included his family – his brother held land at Ampney St. Peter and his son at Aldsworth.

Unlike Regenbald most of the inhabitants of Cirencester at this period remain nameless but the details of the Domesday survey enable us to imagine something of their life. Cirencester was a small rural community, typical of many in England. Its population was mainly concerned with the seasonal farming tasks and was counted in hundreds rather than the thousands of its cosmopolitan Roman predecessor, Corinium.

WHAT TO SEE

● Finds from the Anglo-Saxon period, including the skeleton of one of the warriors found at the Barton, are on display in the Corinium Museum, Park Street.

Cirencester in 12th and 13th Centuries: the Abbey gains control

Today there are few visible reminders of the great Augustinian Abbey of St. Mary which dominated the landscape and the lives of the people of Cirencester for over 400 years. One of the principal gateways, Spitalgate, survives, known locally as the Norman Arch. Part of the boundary wall of the Abbey precinct can be seen in Gosdith Street and the lake in the Abbey Grounds was once the Abbey's fishpond. Some of the more famous abbots – Blake, Hakeburn, Hereward and Estcote – are commemorated in the names of the modern roads which now lie on their domain while the site of the Abbey church is marked by a plaque placed by Cirencester Civic Society.

The Abbey was the biggest of the five Augustinian houses founded by Henry I (1100–1135). Revived on the continent in the tenth century as a means of combatting clerical laxity, the Augustinians were regular canons who followed a monastic rule. They were an order especially favoured by Henry.

Traditionally it is thought that work began on the Abbey in 1117 and the building must have been sufficiently advanced for the consecration in 1130 or 1131 of the first Abbot, Serlo, formerly Canon and probably Dean of Salisbury. With him would have come the nucleus of the community – perhaps some twelve canons in all – from Merton Priory.

In 1133 Henry I's charter endowed the Abbey with a great complex of lands, almost all of which are described as belonging to the tenure of Regenbald (see chapter 3). Regenbald himself, known to have been in the service of Edward the Confessor in 1050, is unlikely to have been still alive at this time. As a cleric his property at his death would normally have reverted to the Crown but it could have been set aside, by special royal favour for a religious foundation in an area where he had family associations. Evidence deduced from taxation records contained in the Pipe Rolls of 1129 suggests that most of his Gloucester-

Abbey site Excavations. Foundations of Saxon apse, looking east (curving wall) with Roman walls beneath cut by construction of Saxon apse. Upright stones (rectangle) in foreground represent the tomb of Regenbald?

Courtesy Cirencester Excavation Committee.

shire properties were already in the hands of the Church of St. Mary which the Abbey was about to supersede. Presumably these would have been donated with royal permission sometime after the Domesday survey of 1086. The total value of these possessions was 21¼ hides and comprised the churches of Preston, Driffield and Ampney St. Mary and land in these parishes and at Norcote and Elmstone. All these were now transferred to the Abbey with Regenbald's other estates – in Gloucestershire, the church at Cheltenham; in Wiltshire, the churches of Latton, Eisy, Pewsey and Avebury; in Berkshire, the churches of Cookham, Bray, Hagbourne and Shrivenham; in Somerset, the churches of Frome, Wellow and Milborne Port; in Dorset, the church of Pulham and in Northamptonshire, the churches of Rowell and Briggstoke. In addition there was land in Oxfordshire and houses at Cricklade and Winchester.

However, the Abbey was not able immediately to enjoy the entire revenue from this beneficence as some parts appear to have been in the possession of others on a lifetime basis. Their interests were protected as were those of the secular canons, specifically mentioned in the charter who had hitherto served the Church. Regenbald was obviously regarded by the Abbey as a major benefactor – from the time of Abbot Richard (1187–1213) the canons were allowed to celebrate his anniversary by partaking of two dishes of meat and two draughts of wine and providing food for 100 poor people. The tomb of Regenbald, tradition had it, was in the Abbey – John Leland, in the 1530's, reported that he had seen a tomb with a cross of white marble, bearing an inscription to this effect. Dr. Evans has pointed out that this cross was unlikely to have been earlier than the fifteenth century since white marble was a very costly material which was rarely used in church monuments before the Renaissance. However, during the 1965 and 1966 excavations a tomb was discovered in the centre of the nave of the Abbey church, thought to be of an earlier date than the late twelfth century when this part was built and suggesting that it might have been preserved from a previous church on the site. As the tomb had been cut into the filling of an abandoned crypt thought to date from no later than the ninth century because of its ring construction it must either have belonged to the second Saxon church on the site, if that existed, or to the post-Conquest period.

Henry I also granted the Abbey the two hides of land in Cirencester, the small property at Painswick and the third of the

The surviving gate of the Abbey – an early twentieth century photograph.
Courtesy Bingham Library.

tolls of the market which had belonged to the Church at the Domesday survey. To this the King added two thirds of the royal demesne, the sheriff's hide for gardens and a mill and the wood of Oakley, reserving for the Crown the hunting rights and the right of making assarts (clearings).

The Abbey was thus handsomely endowed but although royal patronage continued for many years most of its wealth was always derived from its original foundation. It found few benefactors among the nobility – in 1155 Roger, Earl of Hereford gave two hides in Cirencester and in 1156 Roger de Clare donated demesne tithes in Rothwell but neither of these grants was excessively generous. About 1200 a small amount of land in County Kerry, Ireland, was acquired from Henry I's illegitimate grandson, Meiler Fitz Henry. Perhaps, understandably, local gentry and the rising middle classes were more favourably disposed – for example, Richard Murdac gave the canons five acres of land in Baunton and Constance Musard, sister of Hasculf Musard, Lord of Miserden, gave them lands at Chesterton and Siddington.

From the thirteenth century onwards property was often acquired by lease – such as the manor of Wiggold for ten years in 1242 – or purchase – such as the house of one Robert Lente in the Market Place for ten marks. Those entering the religious life would sometimes bring land as their premium. In this way the Abbey acquired land in Redcliffe Street, Bristol when Matthew Lewin of Brislington, Bristol joined the community.

The number of canons in the community seems to have fluctuated from twenty to the maximum of forty (said to have been present at the election of a new Abbot in 1307). Until after the Black Death there would have been in addition an unknown number of lay brothers who undertook many of the domestic duties. These too would have brought land or property when they entered. Few details of the internal life of the community or the management of its estates survive but the order to which they belonged demanded from the canons adherence to a routine of prayer and study as well as offering them opportunities to use talents in such offices as Almoner, Hosteller, Cellarer or Infirmarian. In certain circumstances they could serve the churches under the Abbey's jurisdiction, they sometimes represented the Abbey as legal attorneys and they superintended the administration of its estates. In their black furlined cassocks and black hoods, the canons would have been a not unfamiliar sight to the people of Cirencester.

The first part of the Abbey complex to have been built would have been the church itself. Until the domestic ranges of the cloister were erected the Abbot and the canons would probably have lived in temporary quarters. To assist the building Henry I gave them freedom from tolls and dues on all materials but progress must have been impeded by the civil war between Stephen and Matilda which followed Henry's death in 1135. Gloucestershire saw much of the fighting at this time since Miles of Gloucester, Constable of Gloucester Castle and Sheriff of the county, transferred his allegiance to Matilda when she landed from Normandy in 1139. Matilda fortified the castle in Cirencester, which according to the contemporary chronicler of Gesta Stephani, was 'close to the holy Church of the Religious like another Dagon to the Ark of the Lord God'. In 1142 after burning Wareham in Dorset, Stephen marched northwards and taking Cirencester by surprise 'he gave it to the flames and razed to the ground the rampart and the outworks'. This is the only documentary reference to Cirencester castle. The present con-

Cirencester Parish Church with Abbey House in the background.

Photo. H. Wingham.

sensus of opinion is that it was in the area of the present Mansion in Cirencester Park. Castle Street is a medieval street name and joins the supposed site to the Market Place. Park Lane was formerly known as Law Ditch – possibly the moat surrounding the castle motte. The township boundary excludes this area – like the Abbey, the castle would have been a law unto itself.

Following Stephen's death in 1154, Henry II, son of Matilda, became king without difficulty. Like his grandfather Henry I, he favoured Cirencester Abbey, granting it in 1155 the revenues of the royal vill of Cirencester for the continuation of the building work. The vill or township was the inhabited area of the ancient royal demesne and its boundaries are not clear. The recorded evidence of stone crosses – the customary medieval method of marking boundaries – at three points in the present London Road, near the bridge over the Churn, at the southern end of Cricklade Street and at the junction of Sheep Street and Castle Street – give some indication. The present Querns Lane and Lewis Lane formed the southern extremity and the line of Sheep Street (before the modern development of Phoenix Way) and

36

Park Lane was the western boundary. It took in the present Cecily Hill down to the Gunstool Brook, then followed the River Churn along Cripps Mead, the back of Thomas Street and Gloucester Street to the 'Gilden' Bridge. From there it ran back along the east side of Gloucester Street, Dollar Street and Gosditch Street, excluding the Abbey precinct, behind the Parish Church and the back of Dyer Street, probably following the river along the Abbey boundary Wall.

Despite Henry II's generosity it was not until October 1176 that the Abbey church was dedicated at a splendid ceremony in the presence of the king himself and four bishops. The Abbey church was probably still unfinished for eleven years later the Abbey accounts record £7 7s 0d for roofing the church and repairing the workshops. Masons and carpenters would find employment for many more years on the site.

The Abbey church overlapped the site of the pre–Conquest parish church and it would have been possible for the latter to have been used by both parishioners and canons as a temporary measure until it was necessary to demolish it for the construction of the Abbey nave. However, architectural historians date the first building on the site of the present parish church of St. John the Baptist from about 1120, suggesting that its construction may have proceeded concurrently with that of the Abbey. In the parish church two twelfth century arches survive – one, now an internal doorway leading from St. Catherine's Chapel to the Lady Chapel, was originally an external entrance through the north wall of the chancel arch, perhaps affording a convenient access to the Abbey. About 1180 the chancel was widened on the south side only, throwing it out of centre with the chancel arch and the nave. Two arches were opened in the new wall and the round piers of this still exist. About 1240 the original Norman nave was widened to its present dimensions and replaced by an Early English nave with pointed arches and lancet windows. Although this in turn would be replaced in the sixteenth century it is possible to discern the line of its roof in the west wall of the north aisle and over the tower arch. At this time the Lady Chapel and the Chapel of St. John the Baptist were added. Beneath the Lady Chapel lay the charnel house where bones of the dead were piled up.

The Abbey and parish church were not the only buildings being erected in Cirencester during this period. The hospital of St. John the Evangelist, in Spitalgate Lane has been dated from

The remains of St. John's Hospital, Spitalgate. *Photo. A. Welsford.*

the architectural evidence of the surviving part of the nave arcade as belonging to the reign of Henry II. However, its foundation is ascribed to Henry I in 1133 since the townsmen of Cirencester in 1343 claimed that the King in that year had allocated to it the remaining third of the tithe from the royal demesne and three cartloads of underwood weekly from the forest of Oakley for the hospital to care for the destitute and sick. The canons were said to have appropriated the hospital at a later date, asserting that it had been founded and built by their predecessors and that the inmates were supported by the alms of the faithful and a daily distribution of food by the abbey's almoner according to ancient custom. This appropriation gained the papal confirmation in 1222 and royal approval in 1348.

It was also later alleged that the Abbey had appropriated the other medieval Cirencester hospital – the hospital of St. Lawrence founded in the middle of the thirteenth century by the lady of the manor of Wiggold, Edith Bissett, on land she held of the Crown, on the corner of Gloucester Street and Barton Lane. The hospital was supposedly for lepers although in medieval times the term leprosy could be applied to any skin disease. It seems that Abbot William Hereward converted the hospital into an almshouse for two women at the beginning of the fourteenth century – a deed confirmed by Edward III in 1343. Nothing remains of the original building – the present almshouses on the site were rebuilt about 1800.

Henry II's lease of the vill of Cirencester ceased with his death in 1189 but his successor Richard I's need of money to fund the third crusade was turned to the Abbey's advantage. In 1189 for a rent of £30 per annum the King granted the Abbey the town and manor of Cirencester in perpetuity together with the lordship of the Seven Hundreds. The Seven Hundreds were part of late Saxon organisation which, with certain adaptations, continued as units of local government in the medieval period. By 1189 the Seven Hundreds were in fact administratively only six – Long-tree, Rapsgate, Brightwell's Barrow, Bradley, Crowthorne and Minety, and the urban township of Cirencester. These repre-sented an area encompassing the river valleys of the Leach, lower Coln and Churn and the plateau between the Frome and the Wiltshire Avon, taking in growing settlements such as Tetbury and Fairford. The Abbot could exercise considerable power over this territory through the hundred courts which all freeholders were obliged to attend as jurors although probably the lordship did not bring great financial rewards.

The Abbot's control was further strengthened when King John in 1203, in return for another £100 and the promise of a palfrey, allowed him the privilege of excluding the Sheriff, the King's representative and instrument of the King's courts, from the territory of the Seven Hundreds except for pleas of the crown. In future the Sheriff would deliver the King's summons from the Exchequer to the Abbot who would collect the dues and make his own returns. In 1222 Henry III granted the Abbot permission to build his own gaol and gallows for use when any belonging to the Abbot's jurisdiction were condemned by the King's justices. These facilities the Abbot obligingly lent his friends – the Abbot of Pershore on occasions borrowed the Cirencester gallows if a man from his Cowley manor was to be hanged. The Abbot's right was jealously guarded since he could claim the felon's goods – hence his anger against Elias Giffard of Brimpsfield who erected his own gallows instead of bringing men to Cirencester.

As their feudal lord the Abbot exercised even greater authority over his own manorial tenants. All disputes over tenure, debt and distraint and minor law and order offences were tried according to the custom of the manor. Fines, confiscation of goods, the pillory, stocks and ducking stool were amongst the penalties levied. The Gunstool Brook was probably the site of the

Stone figures of a Pope and an Abbot from the Abbey.

Courtesy Corinium Museum.

ducking stool since Gunstool is a corruption of 'gongstool', a medieval name for ducking stool. The pillory and stocks stood in the Market Place. Not all the tenants accepted the situation – in 1302 Thomas Matyshale having had some of his cattle destrained by the Abbot for default of service tried to bring the case to the King's court. He was unsuccessful since he was the Abbot's tenant and, as the Abbot's counsel said, 'neither in this court or elsewhere are we going to make any answer to the common law of England'.

From his customary tenants – those who held their land in return for service – the Abbot could exact much. Depending on the terms of their occupation their work ranged from working one day a week throughout the year on the Abbot's lands to ploughing, mowing or carrying hay and corn at specific periods. 'None is so free that he must not plough and carry with waggon and cart' says a twelfth century document. In this way were maintained the three Abbey farms – the Barton whose dovecote

The Dove Cote, the Barton.   *Courtesy Bingham Library.*

and great barn still survive and the two within the Abbey precinct, the Almery Grange and the Spyringate Grange. The buildings of the latter survived until the nineteenth century. In addition to these services all persons living in the town, males and females, permanent and temporary, were bound to do three days work in making the Abbot's hay and harvesting his corn in return for which they were 'honourably fed'.

A customary tenant had no right to sell or bequeath land – if the land was regranted to his heirs a fine or heriot of the best chattel, often a horse or beast, was levied. On death the second best chattel went to the church as 'mortuary'. In the case of Cirencester tenants the mortuary also went to the Abbot since he was rector of the parish church. When a tenant's daughters married he paid another fine, merchet, to his lord the Abbot.

41

Corn had to be taken to the Abbot's mills for grinding – another source of irritation since both Abbot and miller took a share. A tenant had the right to buy and sell goods (except horses) freely at the weekly market but he paid the Abbot a tax or chepingavel of 2½d twice a year for the privilege.

The Abbey also was subject to financial pressures. In 1195 and 1206 it paid twice as much tax to the Crown as in the whole thirty-five years of Henry II's reign. The situation was not helped by mal-admininstration. The Abbot of the day, Richard, resorted to selling corrodies, the right to enjoy food and lodging at the Abbey in return for a lump sum. Much of the Abbey's affairs at this time seem to have been in the hands of one Jordan who was probably dishonest as well as inefficient. A joint visitation from the Archbishop of Canterbury, Hubert Walter and the Bishop of Worcester, resulted in changes. The Abbot was not to act without the advice of three of the canons who would take responsibility for the finances. For any major business the Abbot was to consult 'Master Alexander'.

The 'Master Alexander' thus named was probably Alexander Nequam who himself became abbot in 1213. Nequam was one of two notable scholars at the Abbey in the first century of its existence, the other being Robert of Cricklade, afterwards Prior of St. Frideswide's, Oxford. Nequam, born and educated at St. Albans, had been a distinguished teacher at the University of Paris before entering the Cirencester community. He was a prolific and renowned author on many subjects, ranging from a Latin grammar book for children to the great De Naturis Rerum, a contemporary view of science. Doubtless his works were among the growing number of manuscripts housed at first in a cupboard (armarium) in a wall of the Abbey cloister and later in proper bookstores. By the end of its life it seems that the Abbey had a working library which would have contained, on the evidence of lists made in the fourteenth century and at the Dissolution, at least 300 volumes. A few of these survive today in Hereford Cathedral Library, Jesus College Library, Oxford and the British Museum. The canons would have had access to all the major scholarly works, some of which they themselves would have copied. The names of some of these contemporary scribes survive – Jocelin, Simon of Cornwall, Fulco. Interestingly one named was a professional layscribe – Ralph de Pulleham who was employed to work with Alexander the cantor of Cirencester. Although the first recorded mention of a school at the Abbey occurs in 1242, with such facilities it is possible that before this date there would have been a school for the almery boys who acted as servers at masses, as well as for the novices.

Fortunately for the Abbey, Alexander Nequam had the royal favour during the troubled reign of King John. The King was present at his election and when, in 1215, Nequam went to the fourth Lateran Council in Rome, John ordered the bailiffs of Dover to provide him with a ship. Nequam successfully negotiated the restoration of the Seven Hundreds after their confiscation during the Interdict 1208–1214 when much property had been forfeit to the Crown. He gained a decision from the Exchequer that the vill of Cirencester should henceforth be free from tallage (taxation) and a grant from the King for an eight day fair at the Feast of All Saints. The profits of this would have been a welcome addition to the Abbey's revenues. Another Abbot, Roger of Rodmarton, gained a similar concession from Henry III in 1253 for a fair at the feast of St. Thomas the Marytr.

Henry III was one of a number of royal visitors entertained at the Abbey. He came, as a young boy, in 1218, accompanied by the Papal Legate. Edward I in 1282 and Edward II in 1321 kept Christmas in Cirencester. Five years later in 1326, Queen Isabella and the future Edward III were guests of the Abbot. Another mark of royal favour, according to John Leland, occurred in 1261 when Henry III's sister-in-law, Sanchia of Provence, wife of Richard of Cornwall who held the manor of Lechlade, bequeathed her heart for burial in the Abbey with an accompanying legacy of £100.

By the early years of the thirteenth century the domestic buildings in the cloister had reached the stage of being ready for their piped water supply. Water for the lavatorium and reredorter probably came from the Gunstool Brook which flowed through the Abbey precinct. The pure water needed for the refectory range came from a spring at Stratton – the present artificial water course which enters the Abbey precinct at Spital Gate could be part of the conduit which carried it. There was always great concern to gain control of the local watercourses and their mills and by the end of the thirteenth century the Abbey had acquired all three of the mills originally belonging to Cirencester manor at Domesday – Brain's Mill at the Gildenbridge in Gloucester Street and both of the Barton Mills, known at this time as Clerks' Mills.

In the latter years of the thirteenth century there was again evidence of mal-administration. In 1276 the prior, William Haswell was accused of being a drunkard and of squandering Abbey revenue on his kinsfolk. However, the building work continued. In 1292 a Papal Indulgence was granted to those donating money for this purpose and by 1309 the chancel of the Abbey church had been extended and three new chapels were in position. The Abbey was also acquiring property in the town. Evidence from the fines for the breach of the Statute of Mortmain of 1279 which forbade the transfer of land to ecclesiastical bodies, shows that over a hundred such transactions had taken place between 1279 and 1307. Such obvious increasing influence would inevitably lead to resentment amongst the inhabitants and before long this found open expression.

WHAT TO SEE

• The Norman Arch (leading from Abbey Grounds to Abbey Way) – a gateway of the Augustinian Abbey.

• St. John's Hospital, Spitalgate – surviving part of the arcade of the Hall.

• Examples of sculptures and masonry from the Abbey – Corinium Museum, Park Street.

• The site of the Abbey church is shown by a plaque erected by Cirencester Civic Society on the stone balustrade in front of the present Abbey House flats.

Cirencester 1300–1485: Abbey versus Town

Cirencester's medieval origins are discernible in the medieval names of some of the streets in daily use by its modern inhabitants. Castle Street, leading to the castle, Gosditch Street (which in medieval times took in Black Jack Street and Park Street) a corruption of Goggesditch or Gooseditch Street, Dollar Street from the Dolehall or Almery Gate of the Abbey where food or 'dole' was dispensed to the poor, Cricklade Street, leading to Cricklade, and Dyer Street, a name in use from 1348, arising from the dyers who lived there, which gradually replaced the older Chepingstrete (from cheping = market). Other medieval streets

The Weavers' Hall, Thomas Street. A nineteenth century print.
Courtesy Bingham Library.

Monmouth House and the bridge at the foot of Cecily Hill — a nineteenth century print.   *Courtesy Bingham Library.*

are still recognisable under different names. Coxwell Street, renamed in the seventeenth century after a wealthy family who lived there, was originally Abbot's Street. Thomas Street is the medieval Battel Street which was later called after St. Thomas' Hospital which stood there. For a similar reason Gloucester Street was known as St. Lawrence Street because of the hospital of St. Lawrence which stood on the corner of Barton Lane. Cecily Hill existed as Inchthrop or St. Cecilia's Street and Spitalgate Lane appears as Raton Rowe. Sheep Street was Shoterstrete, possibly a reference to the site of the archery butts. Querns Lane was known as Newstrete and Lewis Lane, originally called the Fosse, by the thirteenth century seems to have become Lewis Lane, possibly from the meadows to the south of it, owned by Richard de Lewes. Little medieval building apart from the parish church survives. The Weavers' Hall in Thomas Street is possibly the earliest secular building left in Cirencester. Monmouth House, also in Thomas Street, is a Tudor restoration of a fourteenth century building and the old Grammar School building in Park Lane is known to have medieval features. The medieval High Cross, which once stood at the head of the Market Place can be seen near the west door of the parish church. The cross was removed from the Market Place in the eighteenth century because of its delapidated condition and placed in

46

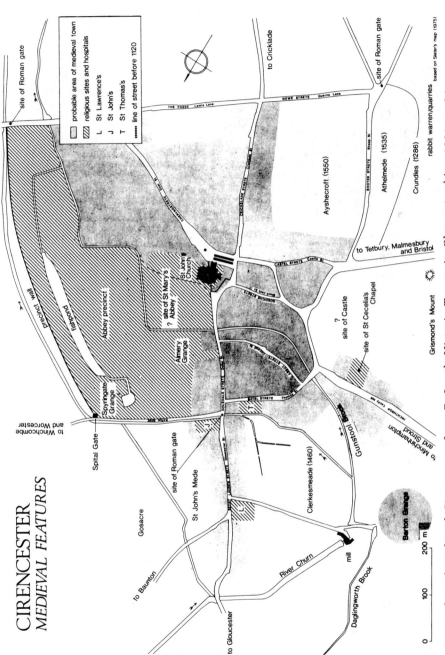

CIRENCESTER
MEDIEVAL FEATURES

Legend:
- probable area of medieval town
- religious sites and hospitals
- L St Lawrence's
- J St John's
- T St Thomas's
- line of street before 1120

site of Roman gate

to Winchcombe and Worcester

precinct wall

fishpond

Abbey precinct

Spryngate Grange

Spital Gate

Gosacre

to Baunton

St John's Mede

site of Roman gate

to Gloucester

River Churn

Daglingworth Brook

mill

Clerkesmeade (1460)

Amery Grange

site of St Mary's Abbey

St John's Church

Gunstool Brook

site of Castle ?

site of St Cecelia's Chapel

to Minchinhampton and Stroud

Grismond's Mount

Barton Grange

CASTEL STRETE Castle St

GOSDICHE STRETE

THE FOSSE Lewis Lane

NEWE STRETE Querns Lane

SHOTER STRETE Sheep St

Aysecroft (1550)

Athelmede (1535)

Crundles (1286)

rabbit warren/quarries

site of Roman gate

to Cricklade

to Tetbury, Malmesbury and Bristol

INCHTWOOR Cecily Hill

based on Slater's map (1975)

0   100   200 m

Street plan of Medieval Cirencester, from R. Leach *Historic Towns in Gloucestershire*, 1981, p. 24.

Cottages at City Bank, Watermoor, the surviving remains of Langley's Mill buildings. *Photo. A. Welsford.*

Cirencester Park. It was returned to its present position in 1927.

The streets themselves would have been narrow, dark, dirty and noisy. Open watercourses, often polluted with household rubbish, ran through many of them. Some of these watercourses were still open, many centuries later. In 1780 a channel four or five foot deep running the entire length of Gloucester Street was filled in at the expense of Samuel Blackwell, one of the town's two M.Ps. The branch of the River Churn which flowed between Black Jack Street and south of Coxwell Street was only covered in 1854. Beyond these streets lay meadows and pastures and common grazing ground. Although the Abbot had taken over the Querns or Crundles (meaning quarries) in 1286, thus preventing its use by the townspeople, they still continued to use Watermoor Common, just outside the old Roman defences, and King's Mead. Watermoor at this time was a sub-manor of Chesterton, originally named after the de More family who occupied it.

Although small by modern standards with a population of probably no more than 2,500, by the fourteenth century Cirencester was an increasingly important centre of trade. A list of market tolls of 1321 enumerating some 80 items which could be bought and sold, includes cattle, horses, goats, bean and pea meal, cheese, butter, fish, salt, alum, iron, lead, tin, brass, linen,

48

The medieval High Cross, removed from the Market Place in the eighteenth century and restored to its present position in 1927.   *Photo. J. Welsford.*

silk and cloth with gold – evidence of a thriving community with sophisticated demands. By the fourteenth century, also, Cotswold wool was eagerly sought by merchants from Northern France, Flanders and Florence. Italian merchants who knew Cirencester were more than willing to buy wool in advance – particularly from the Abbey which was able to profit from the flocks of Cotswold sheep which were reared on the hill pastures

49

in its possession. Foreign merchants settled in the town – such as Giles and Henry Beaupyne whose descendant Thomas, although Mayor of Bristol in 1383, was buried in Cirencester Abbey in 1403. By 1341, ten wool merchants are known to have been in business here and two hundred years earlier in the reign of Henry II, references to Ralph the Weaver, Henry the Dobber (Dyer) and Norman the Fellmonger show that woollen manufacture was being undertaken. By the mid-fourteenth century Cirencester had ousted Winchcombe as the principal centre of Cotswold wool before its export through London, Bristol or Southampton. The wool sales took place in the great Boothall where the Corn Hall now stands. Nearby was the centre of another flourishing trade – the Saltwiche – dealing in a valuable and essential commodity of medieval times. Salt probably reached Cirencester from Droitwich by several routes or saltways of which the ancient track, the Whiteway, may have been one.

Amid such obvious signs of prosperity it must have been particularly galling for the townspeople that the conduct of their trade was firmly in the hands of the Abbot. Under royal charter he took the tolls of the weekly market and the profits of the fairs. His steward presided over the Market Court – the Pie-Powder Court – which met in the building in the Market Place known as the Tolsey and was empowered to dispense instant justice by settling disputes and fining offenders. These regulations and other manorial customs while acceptable in an agricultural community grew increasingly irksome as the economy became more dependent on trade and manufacture. There was occasional violent resistance as in 1302, when a number of tenants began to use their own handmills for grinding corn. The Abbot's bailiff broke into houses and either destroyed the mill stones or carried them off to the Abbey. An attempt to indict the Abbot before the King's justices at Gloucester only resulted in twenty men having to admit that they had made a false claim and a fine of 100 marks.

In 1343 such quarrels and litigation culminated in a petition from the townspeople to Edward III. Amongst the long list of grievances were charges that the Abbot had administered the Hospitals of St. John and St. Lawrence to his own advantage, that he had destroyed all the venison in Oakley Forest, and had enclosed sixty acres of common pasture at the Querns. He was said to have encroached upon the King's highway by building in the Market Place – the origin of the three streets at the top which remained as a reminder of the Abbey's influence until the early nineteenth century. Moreover the townsmen claimed that Henry I had given them a charter to have free customs as burgesses and that Cirencester was a borough belonging to the King who ought to receive £100 a year from it in taxes. Unfortunately they were only able to produce a copy of this charter, asserting that a former prior William de Clerband had obtained the original by false pretences and burnt it. Amongst the twenty men who testified to all these charges were some of the principal inhabitants, including William Erchebaud whose family had held a sub-manor for nearly two hundred years. The consensus of opinion, however, seems to be that the copy charter was probably a forgery – it was written in a style not used till the time of Richard I and if it was genuine it seems strange that it had not been produced at the time of the Inquisitions of John and Henry III.

The Abbot was able to produce earlier royal pardons for some of his misdeeds – from 1314 for encroaching on the Market Place and from 1316 for enclosing part of the Querns (Crondles) which he had turned into a rabbit warren. The charges concerning the suppression of the borough were never fully explored. In September 1343 by what looks suspiciously like a bribe, the King himself dismissed all the proceedings against the Abbey by royal writ and granted a charter which confirmed its privileges on all essential points 'on account of the devotion which we bear and have for the glorious Virgin Mary . . . as well as by a fine of £300 which the Abbot and convent have made with us'. The townsmen were fined for false presentment.

Did a borough actually exist? Certainly Cirencester seems often to have been regarded as a borough for taxation purposes but the words 'borough' and 'vill' seem interchangeable in official documents. Between 1294 and 1336 in parliamentary tax returns Cirencester is six times termed a 'borough' and five times a 'vill'. Cirencester was a manor of royal demesne and as such its tenants possessed some of the attributes which resembled those of burgesses such as a liability to pay royal tallage (or tax). The series of royal Inquisitions dating back to Henry II emphasise the manorial character of Cirencester and the villein status of its inhabitants. What is of significance is the townsmen's conviction that there *had* once been a borough and their determination to achieve the privileges of self-government with a mayor and corporation of which they felt they had been cheated. Such status, however, though granted to other towns of similar size and character, always eluded them. There were still occasional outbreaks of resentment – in 1385 'unheard of things' were done to the Abbot and the canons – but for the moment the desire to be independent in something probably led to the foundation of the great Trinity Guild, a social and religious association which could meet for its twice-yearly feasts without the presence of the Abbot's bailiff. There are also references in contemporary documents to similar associations such as the Fraternity of Jesus and the Guild of St. Clement.

The Abbot who successfully dealt with the recalcitrant townsmen was William Hereward. Having cleared the debt he had inherited from his predecessor in 1335, he embarked on an ambitious building programme. As well as additional buildings in the precinct, a Lady Chapel was constructed on the south side of the chancel of the Abbey church and he was probably also responsible for the remodelling of the Chapter House and the provision of the bookstores which were the precursor of the Abbey library. William Hereward's achievements were rewarded by his commemoration in a chantry chapel in the Lady Chapel he had founded. Towards the end of William Hereward's life in 1351 there were again reports of laxity and mismanagement but before his death, in the following year, the Abbot had ensured that the building work could continue. He secured from the Pope, Clement VI, a remission of a year and forty days enforced penance for all who helped. It may have been to take advantage of this opportunity that the Black Prince came to Cirencester in 1353 and was granted a daily Chantry Mass in the Lady Chapel. By the end of the fourteenth century, therefore, it is likely that at the east end of the Abbey church the north aisle had been rebuilt and the choir remodelled to take new choir stalls.

The Black Death of 1348–9 and its aftermath must have interrupted the building although there is no direct evidence of its effects on the population in Cirencester. In a letter written by the Black Prince in 1360 to the Bishop of Salisbury requesting that Cirencester Abbey be allowed to appropriate the revenues of Hagbourne in his diocese, there is reference to the 'impoverishment of the canons after the late common mortality of men'. One of the consequences of the Black Death was a shortage of labour and the Abbot was, therefore, probably even stricter in exacting the customary services from his tenants, although some of these were, by this time, being commuted for money payments.

In 1378 the Bishop of Worcester came once more to Cirences-

The Distribution of Bucks and Does from Braydon Forest – an artistic impression by John Beecham. *Courtesy Bingham Library.*

ter Abbey to investigate its mal-administration. He ordered the almoner, the precentor and the keeper of the parish church to be removed from office. In future, revenues were to be paid only to the treasurer, and the cellarer was to provide good fish, beer and bread. Even this does not seem to have settled the problem completely because some twenty years after this the Abbots of Lanthony Secunda and Oseney were ordered to investigate the disorders at Cirencester. It is perhaps surprising in view of such events that, on New Year's Day 1379, the Pope raised the Abbot, then Nicholas of Ampney, to the status of a bishop. Cirencester thus became a mitred Abbey – the first such grant to an Augustinian house in England since Henry II had gained the distinction for his foundation at Waltham Abbey.

Not long after this there came an opportunity for the townspeople to improve their circumstances. The Earls of Kent and Salisbury rebelled against the King, Henry IV, in 1400 and arrived in Cirencester with their followers in an attempt to raise more supporters. They were captured by a crowd of inhabitants although they tried to distract attention by setting fire to houses and buildings. The Earls were lodged in the Abbot's gaol and next day, without apparently any opposition, the men of Cirencester executed them in the Market Place and sent their heads to the King. Suitably grateful, Henry IV allowed the inhabitants to keep the contents of the treasure chests which had been in the Earls' possession and rewarded the town with an annual grant of deer from the royal forest of Bradon and wine from Bristol. The town bailiff, John Cosyn, received an annual pension of 100 marks.

Basking in royal favour, the townsmen now determined to press their advantage. Raising £600 to support their cause, they complained to the King of the past usurpations of the Abbots and for the next two years while the case was pending, they witheld all their manorial services. Nothing further seems to have been heard of this petition so in 1402 a second petition was presented – this time for the grant of a guild merchant which would give the town control of its trade. Despite the evidence given in Gloucester by twelve knights of the shire that such a grant would contravene existing royal charters, the King acceded to their request. For the next few years relations between town and Abbey were extremely strained. The Abbot's land was neglected and his officers were attacked and beaten if they attempted coercion. On the accession of Henry V in 1413, the Abbot

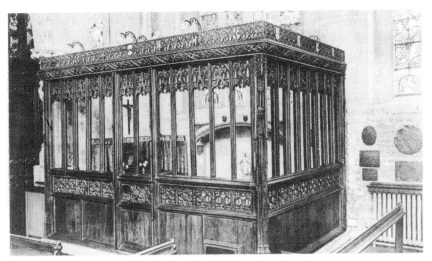

The Garstang Chapel, Cirencester Parish Church. *Courtesy Corinium Museum.*

obtained a fresh exemplification of his rights and the townsmen were forced to return to their ancient obedience. Thirty-one customary tenants and seventy-four town dwellers 'for aiding and abetting' were tried at Gloucester. A total of £6,000 damages was awarded to the Abbot and in 1418 the guild merchant charter was repealed.

Once again thwarted in their efforts to achieve a measure of self-government, the wealthy men of Cirencester now turned their attention to beautifying their parish church. With the rewards from Henry IV work had already begun on the tower soon after 1400. It had been intended to add a spire but because of settlement they were forced to build two spur buttresses to support the tower when it was finished. The Garstangs, wealthy wool merchants, originally from the north of England, built a chantry chapel to St. Edmund of Canterbury. This housed the tomb of Henry Garstang on which can be seen his coat of arms and merchant's mark. Two Cirencester men, members of the household of the Duke of York – Richard Dixton and William Prelatte, built the chapel of the Holy Trinity, marked on the apex of each arch with the Yorkish badge of falcon and fetterlock. Dixton and Prelatte were also members of the Weavers' Guild of the Holy Trinity and the chapel came to have a special association with the Guild. Here can be found the memorial brasses of

Reginald Spycer
and his four
wives,
Margaretta,
Juliana,
Margarita,
Johanna.

A.D.
1442.
Cirencester.

Hic iacent Regnaldus Spycer quondam Alderman isti ville qui obijt tercio die Julij Anno dni millimo
CCC XLijo et Margareta Juliana margareta et Johanna uxores ei quaes animabus propicietur ds Amen.

The brass of Reginald Spycer, Cirencester Parish Church.
Courtesy Bingham Library.

these two founders and of merchant Reginald Spycer, one of the
prime movers of the events of 1440, with his four wives. Another
merchant's brass is also here – Robert Pagge, with his wife, six
sons and eight daughters 'beloved of all, a peaceful man of trade'.
All these bear silent witness to the wealth and influence of these
fifteenth century citizens.

Many left additional gifts to the church such as Henry Garstang's bequest of a gold and silver pall for use in burials and all
the timber in his meadow near the Foss. The less well off too
made their offerings – an extant inventory of the Lady Chapel of
the parish church (rebuilt in 1450) lists articles such as a 'bride's
veil of cotyn', legacy of Alice Sende and a pair of beads of amber
with a ring of gold and a brooch of silver from Janet Batyn. Other
benefactors used their wealth to improve facilities in the town as
well. John Chedworth, Bishop of Lincoln, in addition to extending St. Catherine's Chapel by founding the chantry of St. Catherine and St. Nicholas, in 1458 gave land to Winchcombe Abbey to
pay an annual salary of £10 to a chantry priest and schoolmaster
for the chantry of St. Mary in Cirencester parish church. This is
usually taken to be the beginning of Cirencester's Grammar

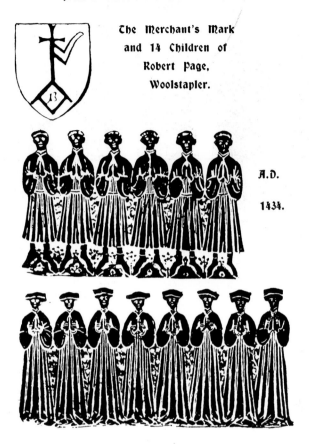

From a Brass in Cirencester Church.

The Merchant's Mark and 14 Children of Robert Page, Woolstapler.

A.D. 1434.

The brass of the children of Robert Pagge, Cirencester Parish Church.
Courtesy Bingham Library.

School. The Weavers' Hall or St. Thomas' Hospital was founded by Sir William Nottingham. In his will in 1483 he left land in trust for the benefit of four poor men living in a home he had erected for them in Battel Street. The earliest surviving brass in the church is of his father, also William Nottingham who died in 1427.

By the end of the fifteenth century relations between Abbey and town seemed to have settled at least into a semblance of mutual tolerance — possibly because the townsmen's energies

St. Catherine's Chapel, Cirencester Parish Church.

Courtesy Corinium Museum.

were being channelled into charitable enterprises – possibly also because both merchants and abbot shared a common interest in the increasingly important wool trade. Neither could have suspected that within the first half of the next century the power of the great Abbey would be swept away for ever.

WHAT TO SEE

- Parish Church of St. John the Baptist:
  interior – Garstang Chapel, Trinity Chapel, St. Catherine's
  Chapel. Pulpit.
  exterior – tower and spur buttresses. High Cross by west
  door.

Tudor Cirencester
'The Old Order Changeth'

Cirencester was not directly involved in the Wars of the Roses but, like many other communities, must have hoped that political stability would come with the accession of the first Tudor monarch, Henry VII, in 1485. During this early Tudor period there was another outburst of building activity in both the Abbey and the Parish Church. Between 1515 and 1530 the thirteenth century nave of the Parish Church was virtually demolished and magnificently rebuilt in the late Perpendicular style. Many citizens contributed to the cost and their coats of arms and merchants' marks can be seen on the shields held by winged angels over the capitals of the pillars. John Pratt, a butcher, in 1514 left £11 to the 'myddel yle' that is the nave and £6-13-4d to make 'ye scaffold to ye same works'. A rood loft bearing the figures of Christ on the Cross with the Virgin Mary and St. John on either side was placed high in the chancel arch. The rood screen, the lower part of which survives, was probably not completed till after 1530, since in 1532 Henry Tapper, a merchant, left £20 towards its installation. Abbot William Hereward is reputed to have given St. Catherine's Chapel its beautiful fan vaulted ceiling – one of the bosses bears his mitre and initials and the date 1508. Other bosses show the royal arms of Henry VII and Henry VIII as Prince of Wales. The very tall bases to the piers of the nave pillars indicate that pews were fitted for the congregation – one original survives from which the present pews were copied in nineteenth century restoration work. The modern visitor can still enjoy these glories in this – the largest parish church in Gloucestershire – but the colour which was characteristic of the medieval church has largely disappeared. At this time many of the walls would have been brightly painted with scenes from the lives of the saints and all forty-two windows would have been filled with stained glass. In 1712 Sir Robert Atkyns reported the remains of very fine glass in most of the windows.

Interior of Cirencester Parish Church, showing the sixteenth century nave.
Courtesy Bingham Library.

This was later collected together in the great east and west windows by Samuel Lysons and more recently the medieval glass from the west window was replaced in its original position in the south aisle. Only the fine wineglass-shaped pre-Reformation pulpit which was re-coloured and gilded in 1865 probably retains something of its original appearance.

The exterior of the Church was also embellished. The exterior of the nave was finished with battlements and, as some of these over the east end show the mitre, staff and initials of Abbot William Hereward, he probably assisted in the work. On the string course is the famous Whitsun Ale procession – stone figures with musical instruments. The great south Porch was added between 1490 and 1500. Apparently built on land owned by the Abbey, it was probably used by the canons for secular dealings with Royal Commissioners to keep them out of the Abbey precinct. A number of parishioners seem to have made substantial contributions to its erection. Alys Avening, aunt of Thomas Ruthall, Bishop of Durham who was said to have been a native of Cirencester, gave £66–13–0d in 1501 and Rudder states that Ruthall's mother and others also gave money for the same purpose. The Porch, or Parvise as it was later known, was given

The pre-Reformation wine glass pulpit, Cirencester Parish Church.
Courtesy Corinium Museum.

to the town by the Bishop of Gloucester in 1672 and from then its main room was used as the Town Hall.

The Abbey's own building schemes were equally ambitious. John Leland, visiting Cirencester about 1540, referred to the nave of the Abbey Church as 'but a new work' implying that it had only recently been completed. William of Worcester, a visitor of 1480, noted the measurements of the Abbey Church. It was 245 feet long and 72 feet wide with a Lady Chapel 132 feet long and 38 feet 6 inches wide on the south side of the choir. The length of the cloister was 91 feet. Pieces of fan tracery matching that of the vaulting in St. Catherine's Chapel are said to have been dug up in

South Porch of Cirencester Parish Church – interior.

Courtesy Corinium Museum.

the Abbey grounds and possibly were once part of the cloister roof. Such evidence and the fragments of masonry now in the Corinium Museum give us some idea of the splendour of the great Abbey Church – well over 100 feet longer than the Parish Church with its nave possibly constructed in the same magnificent style as the latter.

Other domestic building projects were undertaken by the last two abbots. The Abbot's house situated between the cloister and the Spitalgate Grange was extended and Abbot John Blake built the 'right goodly clothing Mylle' later known as New Mills. Some of these buildings were in use until the early twentieth century

New Mills in the early twentieth century.   *Courtesy Bingham Library.*

and the mill house survives today. Leland described the mill 'as wonderfully necessary because the town standeth all by clothing'. Cirencester, like many other west country areas, was sharing in the increasingly expanding wool manufacture which from the mid fourteenth century absorbed more and more of the raw wool supplies, although foreign demand remained high. Cloth produced in the west country required fulling – a process, using fuller's earth, in which the cloth is made thick and beaten by water. The mills built by Abbot Blake had three stocks or wooden feet, raised and dropped alternately by a wheel driven by water from the River Churn. This seems to be the first definite mention of such a mill in Cirencester although one is recorded in Gloucestershire as early as 1180 at Temple Guiting. These mills became increasingly numerous in the sixteenth century, particularly in the Stroud Valley area where the plentiful and powerful water supply was an important factor in its domination of the woollen manufacture in later years. New Mills also contained a gig mill worked by water to raise the nap on cloth after fulling.

The Abbot did not long enjoy the fruits of his investment. The matrimonial difficulties of Henry VIII led in the 1530's to the severance of England's ties with the Papacy through the acts of the great Reformation Parliament of 1529–36. In 1534 the King was declared Supreme Head of the Church of England and the Treasons' Act made it treason to deny this. The monastic communities owing allegiance to parent institutions outside England and Wales and possessing wealth which could restore the Crown's ailing finances, were vulnerable. In 1535 Thomas Cromwell evaluated their condition and possessions in the survey known as the Valor Ecclesiasticus. Completed in six months, this was the first major tax record since that of Domesday. Cirencester Abbey, the wealthiest of nearly two hundred Augustinian houses in the country was assessed at an annual income of just over £1,000. The lesser monasteries were dissolved in 1536 and in 1539 came the turn of the great houses. On 19th December Abbot John Blake signed his admission of the King's supremacy and on 31st December the Abbey formally surrendered. Apart from the Abbot there were then 17 canons in the community. All were provided for. The abbot received an annual pension of £200, sufficient to enable him to live as a country gentleman in Fairford until his death. The prior, Richard Woodall, and the cellarer, William Warbot, received pensions of £13-6-8d and £8 respectively. The others received £6-13-4d except Richard Lane whose annual income was set at £5-6-8d. One canon, William Philipps (or Phelps), received no pension but was to continue as vicar of the Parish Church for his lifetime with an income of £13-6-8d. Out of this he had to pay three chaplains to assist him and provide wine and candles.

There is no evidence of any overt support in Cirencester for the monastic community – perhaps not surprising in view of past relations between the Abbey and the town. The King's Commissioners surveyed the buildings, ordering those deemed 'superfluous' to be destroyed so that the visible signs of monasticism would be obliterated. The church, the chapter house, refectory, dormitory, library, infirmary, kitchen and many of the quarters of the abbey officers were doomed. Other buildings which might be of use to future tenants – the abbot's house, the bakery, brewery and malting houses, the woolstore by the mill and the barns of the Spitalgate and Almery granges – were retained. In charge of the work was Roger Basing, a wine merchant who had previously undertaken tasks for the King. Basing was granted the lease of the site for 21 years. The gold and silver plate and other precious items were sold and the proceeds went to the Crown. Lead was stripped from the roofs, windows and guttering and saved for the King. Fortunately some of the contents of the giant library were rescued by one of the King's Commissioners, Sir John Prise and later found their way into other libraries such as that in Hereford

The Abbey Grounds today. *Photo. A. Welsford.*

Cathedral. Stripped of their roofs the monastic buildings soon fell into decay – a process hastened by the sale of stone to Sir Anthony Hungerford and Robert Strange.

In 1549 Edward VI granted his uncle Thomas Seymour the lordship of the manor of Oakley, the lordship of the Seven Hundreds and the ownership of the Abbey site. After Seymour was convicted of treason, these titles passed to Sir Anthony Kingston. When he died in 1556 under suspicion of treason, all reverted to the Crown. At the beginning of her reign Elizabeth I conferred the Oakley property on her Treasurer, Sir Thomas Parry and in 1564 sold the Abbey site to her physician, Dr. Richard Master for £590-16s-3d. As a further mark of the Queen's favour Dr. Master was given the silver gilt cup which had once belonged to her mother, Anne Boleyn. It sits today in the special safe in the east wall of the Parish Church, displaying Anne's badge of a falcon, holding a sceptre with a rose tree. In 1563 the Parrys sold the Oakley manor to Sir John Danvers. Elizabeth granted him the title together with the lordship of the Seven Hundreds. Soon new houses began to rise on both the Abbey and Oakley sites, bringing welcome employment to craftsmen and tradesmen in the town.

Henry VIII, despite his anti-Papal policy remained doctrinally Catholic and throughout his reign prevented any official acknowledgement of the Protestant views which were gaining

66

Houses in Gloucester Street with stone plinths thought to have come from the Abbey. *Photo. A. Welsford.*

strength among sections of the population and at court. The chantry chapels and their side altars, founded to sing masses for the souls of their benefactors were, therefore, left untouched. Their popularity, at least in Cirencester, seems not to have diminished in the sixteenth century, for several new ones were added. In 1508 John Jones of Duntisbourne gave six houses for masses for his soul for sixty years, after which the money from the rents was to be used for charitable purposes in the town. In 1515 Robert and Elizabeth Richards funded a priest to sing mass at the altar of St. Anthony and to teach two children to sing at divine service there. In 1548, however, the Protestant government of Edward VI dissolved the chantries, pensioned off their priests and diverted their wealth to the King's Exchequer. In Cirencester this meant the loss of priests, the organ player (hitherto financed by St. Christopher's chantry) and choir boys. Only John Jones' chantry seems to have escaped since it had 'not perpetually been devoted to superstitious uses'.

Other changes followed. Statues were removed or mutilated, the rood was taken down and wall paintings were plastered over or white-washed. Cirencester, since Henry VIII's reign, had been part of the newly created diocese of Gloucester to which was appointed as bishop in 1550, the zealous Protestant reformer, John Hooper. At first William Philipps, vicar of Cirencester, adhered to the old Catholic doctrines – on a Sunday in April 1551 he preached a sermon upholding the doctrine of transsubstantiation only to recant publicly the following week in the presence of his bishop being 'most harte sorry for my earore and faulse opinion'. Within two years the situation had been reversed. With the accession of the Catholic Mary Tudor, Bishop Hooper was burned as a heretic in Gloucester, passing through Cirencester on his way, according to Foxe's Book of Martyrs. The dilemmas of their parish priest must also have faced his congregation but Cirencester, like many areas, seems to have acquiesced in the rapid see-saws of the government's religious policies of these years.

When Elizabeth I became Queen in 1558 many hoped for calm but passions aroused by religious controversy were not easily stifled. Elizabeth's policy was to compromise – 'to open windows into no man's soul' but outward conformity was considered essential to the country's safety in face of threats from abroad, her own excommunication by the Pope in 1570 and plots on behalf of the Scottish queen, Mary Stuart. To some those Puritans who desired a separate church seemed as dangerous as the Roman Catholics. Fines for non-attendance at church, whipping, the pillory, imprisonment and occasionally execution were the punishments meted out by the ecclesiastical and civil courts. Occasional references indicate that there were both active Puritans and Roman Catholics in Cirencester although the evidence is insufficient to assess their strength. In 1570 some inhabitants petitioned the Privy Council to take action 'against the tyranny of infected members called Papists'. In 1604 a certain John Chappelin claimed that he had been born in Cirencester and converted to Roman Catholicism by his cousin Thomas Strange, presumably a member of the Strange family of Chesterton since a Mistress Strange of Chesterton appears in a list of recusants (refusers) in 1577. The curate of the parish church, William Aldsworth came in for criticism by the churchwardens in 1573 for his Puritan tendencies. They complained that he did not follow the book of Common Prayer or wear a surplice and that he allowed the congregation to take communion 'some kneeling, some standinge and some sittinge'. A number of Cirencester Puritans came before the ecclesiastical court in Gloucester in 1574, charged with not attending church and refusing to have their children baptised. The authorities appear to have dealt leniently with them for a number of years but now their patience finally ran out. Four of the men were imprisoned in Gloucester Castle for a year but it seems unlikely that the group was deterred. A little later Sir Giles Poole, a local J.P., reported to the Privy Coucil that he had discovered a sect of 'disordered persons assembling together in a desolate place near a wood and appointing their own minister'.

Other problems disturbed the Elizabethan citizen. Inflation was as much a part of life in the sixteenth century as today. It has been estimated that between 1500 and 1603 real wages dropped by 57% while average prices of essential consumables rose by some 488%. Population growth ensured that labour was cheap and wages low. Life cannot have been easy for many of the poorer members of the population but some certainly prospered. Among these were clothiers, the basis of the Gloucestershire woollen industry. A clothier bought raw wool and paid for the spinning, weaving and finishing processes. The brass in the Parish Church of Philip Marner who died in 1587, with long gown, doublet, staff, shears and pet dog is probably a typical illustration of the contemporary prosperous Cirencester clothier, amassing his wealth with care but having a civic responsibility to the less fortunate.

'In Lent by will a sermon he devised
And yerely precher with a noble prised
Seven nobles hee did geve ye poore for to defend
And £80 to XVI men did lend
In Ciseter, Burford, Abingdon and Tetburie
Ever to be to them a stock yerely'

Woolcombers were numerous in Cirencester and carding and spinning were staple occupations for women and children. Weaving was also a home-based craft and many cottages would have had a larger than average room on the ground or first floor to accommodate a loom. Some of the finished cloth might be sold at fairs in Cirencester but much was sent to London by packhorse and waggon. Clothiers were fined if the cloth was not the required length and colour. One Cirencester clothier is recorded as being fined for a piece of blue cloth which was below standard.

Unlike similar towns, Cirencester had no proper guild organisation to regulate manufacture and trade although the written records of the Weavers' Company which exist from 1580 show that this exercised some controls. No loom was to be set up in the town without its licence. The Company also looked after its members – in 1601 3 shillings was paid for Thomas Bradshaw's shroud and 6d for ringing the bells at his funeral. Money had already been given to him in his illness.

There was an attempt at this time to revive the old guild merchant which had existed briefly under Henry IV. Giles Selwin claimed that the Charter had never been properly annulled and persuaded a number of people to support him in the hope that a measure of municipal self government might be achieved. The case was brought in Chancery in 1582. The new lord of the manor, Sir John Danvers was no less opposed to the idea than his predecessor, the Abbot. Prominent citizens such as Christopher George and Robert Strange gave evidence against Selwin and the case was dismissed. Thus was confirmed the manorial organisation which would be part of Cirencester's system of government for another three hundred years. Manorial officials such as constables, ale-tasters, carnals, water bailiffs and two wardsmen or tithingmen from each ward would continue to be appointed when Queen Victoria was on the throne.

Perhaps the pride of some of Cirencester's citizens was a little assuaged by the granting of parliamentary borough status in 1571. All freeholders were now entitled to elect two members – a comparatively small electorate. The first two were Gabriel Blike and Thomas Poole. There was obvious pride too in the town's Grammar School. Deprived, by the dissolution of the Abbey and the Chantries, of annuities which paid the schoolmaster's salary, the townspeople successfully appealed for the continuation of an annual salary of £7 until 1554. When that was stopped under

The Bridges' Tomb, Cirencester Parish Church.   *Courtesy Corinium Museum.*

Mary I, it seems that the schoolmaster was paid out of the John Jones' charity. In 1559 the schoolmaster, William Arderne had his salary restored by the Exchequer and later on the salary was increased to £20 to allow for the appointment of an assistant. Numbers seem to have fluctuated – at its peak in the Elizabethan period they reached about a hundred. During the latter part of the reign when Thomas Helme was in charge they dropped to forty or so. Helme was asked to go because of his 'unscilfulness and slackness' but he obviously held on since there are records of him in the reign of James I. The school by this time was probably in premises in Park Lane, having begun in Dyer Street. The age for entry was seven or eight and boys had to be able to read the English New Testament as a qualification. Although poor children were admitted and taught free, the normal entrance fee for 'towndwellers' was one shilling and for 'outdwellers' three shillings. Tuition fees were another shilling a year. The main subjects were Latin and Greek and boys were expected 'to civillie, courteouslie and duetifully carry and behave themselves'.

Despite its involvement with its own affairs, Cirencester could not be unaware of national events. In 1588 people must have turned out, not without trepidation, as some of the county trained bands, the core of the country's armed forces, passed through the town on their way to the great assembly of troops

71

Old Houses. Market Place. An early nineteenth century print giving an impression of the sixteenth century Market Place.   *Courtesy Bingham Library.*

before the Queen at Tilbury. The Armada had set sail from Spain and the warning beacon fires were ready to light on the Cotswold hills to mark the Spanish invasion. Four years later with the threat from Spain no longer imminent, the townspeople would have flocked to cheer the Queen herself arriving to stay at the new house of Sir John Danvers. The knights and gentlemen of the shire had ridden out to Driffield to escort her and as she entered the town she was greeted with a Latin oration and a 'cuppe of double gilte' worth £20.

The population of the parish at this time probably numbered about 3,000, having been somewhat reduced by a virulent outbreak of plague between 1576 and 1579 when about 500 died. In the first six years of the 1570's burials in the parish churchyard averaged 62 per year. Eighty-three were recorded in 1576, rising to 161 in 1577 and reaching the appalling total of 495 in 1578. The high mortality rate continued into the first three months of 1579. Children were often the most vulnerable – in the peak months of September and October 1578, 115 died and sometimes whole families seem to have been wiped out. The spread of such epidemics was hastened by the poor sanitation of the time – open cesspits, and probably contaminated wells – combined with the cramped and crowded dwellings, in dark and dirty streets in which many must have lived. Little sixteenth century domestic building has survived in the town but it is likely that the wealthier inhabitants would be using stone rather than timber in construction. Generally this was a time when the prosperous extended their houses or built new with a corresponding improvement in domestic comfort, but it is unlikely that many were able to move out of the confines of the medieval town. The new estates of the Masters and the Danvers families were as constricting in this respect as that of their predecesor the Abbot had been.

WHAT TO SEE

- Parish Church of St. John the Baptist:
    interior – the nave, the Boleyn Cup, fan vaulting in St. Catherine's Chapel, the Bridges' monument;
    exterior – the south porch.

- Monmouth House, Thomas Street, a Tudor restoration of a fourteenth century building.
- Gloucester Street, nos. 33 and 35 – timber-framed cottages with plinths of ashlar blocks said to have come from the Abbey.

Seventeenth Century Cirencester
Conflicts and Conflicts Resolved

Within the first half of the new century the people of Cirencester would find barricades in their streets, hear the rattle of musket fire and the thunder of cavalry charges and see men dead and dying as Englishmen fought each other in the great Civil War. Such scenes were probably unimaginable to the inhabitants as they heard in 1603 of the Queen's death and the peaceful accession of the first Stuart King, James I. Nor probably would thoughts of internal strife have been in the minds of the Cirencester men who were called to muster in 1608 by the Lord Lieutenant of the county, as being fit and able to serve in the militia – the country's first line of defence. We can still read their names today in the printed form of the 'Men and Armour' survey compiled from the contemporary manuscript of John Smith of Nibley. Able-bodied men from 20–60 years old appear, classified according to age and stature. They are listed with their occupations in the Cirencester streets where they lived. Some might have failed to attend but the penalties for non-compliance were heavy so it is likely that the group comprised a considerable proportion of the male work force. On this evidence about 18% of these men in Cirencester were involved in the woollen trade and manufacture, including 5 clothiers, 40 weavers, 14 tailors and 6 other associated craftsmen. Leather manufacture was also significant – 22 men were listed as shoemakers and another 10 were glovers.

With many of its population involved in the woollen industry Cirencester would have been affected by the decline caused by competition from lighter worsted cloths and even more in 1614 by the government policy of attempting to retain all broadcloth in England for finishing and dyeing rather than export some for this purpose as had been the usual practice hitherto. Unsold cloth accumulated as foreign markets refused to purchase and although the policy was reversed in 1617, the damage had been

74

Woollen Manufacture and Allied Trades

Clothier	5	
Clothier's Servant	7	
Weaver	40	
Weaver's Servant	2	60
Cardmaker	4	
Dyer	1	
Tucker	1	

Labourer	45	45

Clothing Manufacture/Retail Distribution

Glover	9	
Glover's Servant	1	
Hatter	2	
Mercer	9	
Mercer's Servant	1	41
Draper	4	
Tailor	14	
Tailor's Servant	1	

Food Manufacture and Distribution

Baker	6	
Baker's Servant	1	
Butcher	19	
Chandler	2	
Beer Brewer	1	
Innkeeper	3	39
Tapster	1	
Vintner	1	
Vintner's Servant	4	
Victualler	1	

Leather Manufacture/Allied Trades

Shoemaker	22	
Shoemaker's Servant	3	
Collarmaker	1	
Currier	1	
Sadler	5	33
Sadler's Servant	2	
Tanner	2	
Tanner's Servant	1	
Bookbinder	1	

Building Trades

Carpenter	2	
Glazier	2	
Glazier's Servant	1	
Joiner	6	
Cooper	3	
Mason	6	
Pavier	1	
Plumber	1	29
Carver	1	
Sawyer	2	
Slatter	2	
Wheeler	2	

Agriculture/Horticulture

Gardener	3	
Husbandman	6	
Shepherd	3	
Yeoman	1	15
Hivemaker	1	
Bailiff ?	1	

Care of Horses

Ostler	5	
Smith	8	
Smith's Servant	1	15
Farrier	1	

Transport

Carrier	2	
Carrier's Servant	1	5
Carter	2	

Education/the Arts

Usher	1	
Musician	2	4
Scrivener	1	

Medicine

Apothecary	1	
Barber	2	3

Metal Work

Cutler	2	
Brasier	1	3

Domestic Service

Servants to Gentlemen	12	
Chamberlain	2	39
Servants – unspecified	25	

Miscellaneous

Pedlar	1	
Loiterer	1	
Unclassified	29	

Gentlemen	3	3

Men and Armour 1608 – An analysis of trades and occupations of the men in Cirencester.   *J. Welsford.*

done. In 1622 an official source referred to great poverty among Gloucestershire weavers and large stocks of unsold cloth. Unlike many towns Cirencester had no guild organisation to protect its craftsmen from competition but the Weavers' Company used what authority it had – in 1614 it was agreed that 'no foreign weaver shall set up any loombe but shall pay to the Company £10'.

The care of the poor and sick was the responsibility of the parish. The cost of relief was met by a rate on property owners. Perhaps it was to cope with the increased demands on the parish brought about by the economic crisis that, in 1618, Cirencester appointed an official to control the situation – picturesquely named in the Vestry Book as 'the Biddle of Beggars'. His duties included keeping all strange beggars out of the town and the supervision of the local poor to ensure that the 'wicked poor' able to earn their own living did not receive alms. Children under the age of seven found wandering in the streets were to be set to knitting, spinning or other duties. Private charities or parish funds were used to provide work for adults and apprenticeships for children. The Vestry Book has a list of 53 boys who were apprenticed between 1617 and 1673 under the will of Richard George. Of these 11 were apprenticed to shoemakers and 6 to weavers. Not all stayed in the town – one went to a gunsmith in London, another to a pinmaker in Gloucester. Another benefactor, Sir Thomas Roe, left money in his will for the same purpose.

Many of the well-to-do had a concern for their less fortunate neighbours. Humphrey and Elizabeth Bridges left money and property for the poor and are commemorated in the impressive monument in the parish church – he dressed as a lawyer, she in the formal costume of the early seventeenth century, surrounded by their eleven children. George Monox was another philanthropist whose monument is also in the parish church. Charitable institutions of an earlier age such as St. John's Hospital continued to function. By a 1666 decree of Chancery this was managed by the Vicar, Churchwardens and Overseers of the Poor through their right to appoint the Master.

The Beadle or 'Biddle' of Beggars had other civic duties. He had to prevent parents bringing noisy and crying children to church; to ensure that householders removed 'the muck lying before their houses' and to apprehend those who 'fowle and defyle' the streets as well as capturing straying pigs. Obviously not all Cirencester citizens were careful about their surroundings and the stench of household refuse must at times have been overwhelming. In 1634 Charles Bragge, an innkeeper, built a brewhouse, stable, pigsty and privy in the churchyard, Giles Hancox erected a privy against the tower and Ralph Marchant, together with 33 other people was said to have cast 'filth and nastiness' into the churchyard.

Such irreverent behaviour was not confined to the exterior of the church. In 1614 the duties of the sexton included the 'stilling of noise of children and dogs' in the church and in 1641, William Webb, then sexton, was instructed to shut unruly boys in the vestry or belfry if they caused trouble during the service. Not only children were troublesome. Thomas Parsloe was reported for throwing dirt in church, refusing to take off his hat and 'useing himself irreverently there'. Attendance at church was still compulsory and offenders could be punished. In 1637 three men were said to have gone fishing and several others to have loitered in the streets, throwing snowballs at the time of divine service.

Insistence on church attendance was one aspect of the government's attempt to enforce conformity to the letter of the Book of Common Prayer and to curtail various Puritan practices which had grown up. Archbishop Laud instituted visitations to ensure that the altar stood at the east end of the church and that the Prayer Book was followed. His representative came to Cirencester in 1635 and outwardly at any rate all must have been to his satisfaction for no adverse criticism was made.

Laud's rigorous policies coincided with Charles I's attempts to finance his government without recourse to parliament. Forced billeting of troops on the civilian population was economic for the Crown and in 1628, 300 soldiers descended on Cirencester and had to be quartered at a total cost of £7 a day until they moved on to Gloucester. Even then the town had to provide horses and carts and food for their journey. In the years that followed loans, benevolences and ship money were also collected from the inhabitants. In 1635 Cirencester's assessment for ship money was so high – £53-0-6d – that the sheriff was reluctant to gather it, although eventually the payment was completed.

In peacetime Charles I could keep his head above financial water but the ill-conceived attempts to force the English Prayer Book on the Scots, led to war, an ignominious defeat and the

The overturning of Lord Chandos' Coach in Cirencester Market Place. A painting by John Beecham.   *Courtesy Bingham Library.*

recall of Parliament in 1640. Within two years civil war had broken out to the dismay and bewilderment of many. The causes of the war were complex and are still debated by historians. Although on a minute scale by modern standards, to the ordinary citizen in areas of fighting, the immediate effects were devastating and the inevitable bitterness of the war and its aftermath unforgettable.

On 23rd August 1642, Lord Chandos, Deputy Lieutenant of the county, arrived in the town to issue the Commission of Array to raise troops for the King. He was met with hostility and streets already blocked by chains. Although he had planned to spend the night with Sir William Master at the Abbey, wiser counsels prevailed and he left secretly. The next day his coach was torn apart in the Market Place by an angry mob. Led by prominent citizens such as John George, son of Robert George, Lord of the Manor of Baunton and a member of the Long Parliament, the town declared for parliament although the Pooles of Sapperton, who in 1616 had purchased Oakley Manor from the Danvers, were Royalists.

Cirencester could not be disregarded by the Royalists. Its capture would enable the King to seize Gloucester, open com-

78

munication with his Welsh supporters and complete the defence ring around Oxford, the Royalist headquarters. The town was thought to have natural defences in its stone walls and water courses and under John Fettiplace as civil governor and the Scottish Lieutenant Colonel Carr in charge of military affairs, the garrison, consisting of some trained bands, volunteers, dragoons and two regiments raised by Lord Stamford prepared for the attack. Five sakers (small canon) were at their disposal. Two of these were mounted on the wall of the Oakley Mansion, one in the garden of Abbey House, another in the Market Place and the fifth in the Cricklade Street area 'in George's back side at the south east corner upon Cricklade way'.

Early in January 1643 Prince Rupert arrived. Refusing his demand to surrender, the defenders must have been immensely relieved to see him turn away but relief was short lived. On 30th January Rupert feigned an attack on Sudeley Castle, recently captured for Parliament with the aid of troops withdrawn from Cirencester. Moving away from Sudeley by night the Royalists reached the neighbourhood of the town on 31st January and, during the early hours of Wednesday February 1st, moved within a mile 'giving us alarms all night' as a contemporary recalled. Such alarm might have been even greater had it been known that the Royalists had been re-inforced with troops and two mortars from Oxford.

At noon on Thursday, 2nd February, Rupert launched a two-pronged attack. Leading the main force against the defenders at the Barton House, he dislodged them by sheer force of numbers and pursued them to the barricades at the bottom of Cecily Hill. Breaking through these barriers, the Royalist cavalry were ordered to advance into the town. The defendants ran before them. When they reached the Market Place the Royalists were fired on by snipers from upper windows. Meantime the other Royalist attack had been launched by Lord Carnarvon against the Spitalgate entrance but the defendants fled when they heard that Rupert's troops were in the Market Place. A small brave band held out at Barton Mills and it was during this action that Hodgkinson Paine, a local clothier, fell with the colours in his hand. In the parish church his punning epitaph can still be read:

'He looseing quiet by warre yet gained his ease by it PAINE's life began and paine did cease'.

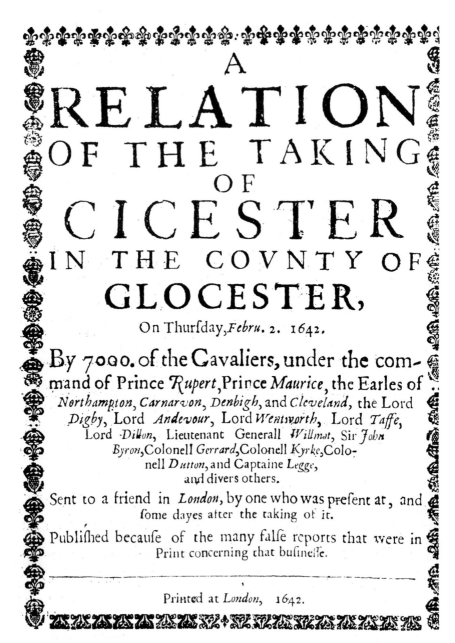

A
RELATION
OF THE TAKING
OF
CICESTER
IN THE COVNTY OF
GLOCESTER,

On Thurſday, *Febru*. 2. 1642.

By 7000. of the Cavaliers, under the command of Prince *Rupert*, Prince *Maurice*, the Earles of *Northampton, Carnarvon, Denbigh*, and *Cleveland*, the Lord *Digby*, Lord *Andevour*, Lord *Wentworth*, Lord *Taffe*, Lord *Dillon*, Lieutenant Generall *Willmat*, Sir *John Byron*, Colonell *Gerrard*, Colonell *Kyrke*, Colonell *Dutton*, and Captaine *Legge*, and divers others.

Sent to a friend in *London*, by one who was preſent at, and ſome dayes after the taking of it.

Publiſhed becauſe of the many falſe reports that were in Print concerning that buſineſſe.

Printed at *London*, 1642.

Cover of a Civil War pamphlet, 1642.　　　Courtesy Bingham Library.

At four o'clock after about four hours fighting Cirencester was in Royalist hands. According to contemporary accounts about 300 defendants were killed and 1,200 prisoners taken. The prisoners were shut up in the church without food or water. Barton Farm was fired and livestock taken from there and the surrounding countryside. Stocks of wool were seized and many houses ransacked. Not even Royalist sympathisers escaped – the lawyer John Plot in Coxwell Street found his house 'full of soldiers and £1,200 taken'. The discovery in 1963 of twelve silver teaspoons dating from 1637–8 between floorboards in business premises, formerly a house in West Market Place suggests that at least one Cirencester citizen was more successful than John Plot in hiding his treasure.

The prisoners including Col. Fettiplace, John George and the Rev. Alexander Gregory were taken to Oxford 'on foot and roped together' in dirt 'sometimes up to their knees'. At Oxford they made an abject submission to the King and were allowed to return home. A Royalist garrison was established in the town under Sir Ralph Dutton. This was surprised later in 1643 by the Earl of Essex but although he took 400 prisoners and seized 30 or 40 waggons of provisions, he could not control the town permanently. Until 1645 the Royalists left Sir Jacob Astley as commander in Cirencester. When he left Colonel Morgan the parliamentary governor of Gloucester took possession of the town.

'O England what did'st thou do, the 30th of this month'. Thus, Alexander Gregory, returned to minister to his flock, recorded the execution of Charles I in 1649, in the Parish Register. For the next eleven years England was a republic and the monarchy, the House of Lords and the Anglican Church were abolished. Another note in the Parish Register illustrates the implications of one of these changes. 'Note that the reason whereof here wanteth severall years for weddings at this time, the Rump Parliament sett forth an Act that all banns should be published three severall market days at the High Cross and the partners to bee married by a Justice of the Peace soe there was but little to be done in Churches'.

In 1660 the monarchy was restored. Charles II entered his capital on 29th May – his thirtieth birthday and the anniversary of his escape after the battle of Worcester. The long silenced bells of the Parish Church resounded through Cirencester in celebration as they have continued to do, with the exception of the war

Coxwell Street which still retains much of its seventeenth century appearance.
Photo. J. Welsford.

years, on the same date ever since. Three years later Charles was himself in Cirencester, en route from Bath to Oxford, as the guest of the Newburghs at Oakley House. Lady Newburgh had been given Oakley House by her father, Sir Henry Poole.

For some the Restoration brought unwelcome change. Alexander Gregory refused to comply with the 1662 Act of Uniformity and subscribe to the revised Book of Common Prayer. He later left the town to live in Minchinhampton as under the Five Mile Act he could not live within five miles of his former curacy. His place as vicar was taken by Thomas Carles. The church, however, had not the power to impose a general conformity and despite attempts to prevent unlawful conventicles, Nonconformist groups in Cirencester, as elsewhere, continued to exist and to increase. The Baptists were already an organised body of about 40, in 1651, under the care of Giles Watkins, a respected tradesman. They now continued their meetings at the house of widow Peltrave in Coxwell Street, possibly the site of their first

The Bear Inn, Dyer Street.   *Photo. A. Welsford.*

chapel which was replaced by the present building in the nineteenth century. A number of weavers were Baptists and services were later also held in the Weavers' Hall. The Presbyterian, later Unitarian, Chapel in Gosditch Street also dates from this period.

The most recorded incidents of harrassment concern the Quakers. Following the visit of George Fox to Cirencester in 1655 and the leadership of John Roberts of Siddington, a determined

The Friends' Meeting House, Thomas Street.　　　　　*Photo. A. Welsford.*

and persisent group maintained their faith in the face of considerable opposition. In 1660 five Friends were sent to prison for
refusing the oath of allegiance and meetings were often broken
up with violence. In 1670 Elizabeth Hewlings, an aged widow,
died of her injuries after being thrown downstairs on one such
occasion. In 1673 a meeting house was built in Thomas Street
and has remained the Friends' Meeting House ever since. Under
the Toleration Act of 1689 both this and the Baptist Chapel were
licensed for worship.

According to an official survey in 1676 there were then 150
confessed Dissenters in Cirencester, about 8% of the total
population. The majority continued to attend the parish church.
Much of the civil as well as the spiritual organisation of the
parish was in the hands of the parish administration. The
accounts of the churchwardens exist from 1666 and show that
there was then an annual income of £80, supplemented by the
poor law rate. The odd items which occasionally occur include
the payment of 6d to three seamen for relief on their journey
(how did they come to be in Cirencester?) and 4d per head for six
fox heads (presumably a reward for extinction of vermin). The
churchwardens also bought or acquired a large quantity of

No. 2, Watermoor Road, thought to be on the site of the former manor house of Chesterton. *Photo. A. Welsford.*

leather buckets – a total of 74 in 1673. Ladders were stored in the church and could be borrowed for a small charge. Such equipment would be available in the event of fire in the town. With no police force, law and order was the responsibility of the Parish Constables who could call on others to assist. Parish officials had to ensure that highways and bridges were kept in good repair. The inhabitants of Watermoor were said to have allowed their section of the road from Cirencester to Cricklade to fall into disrepair and in 1684 the occupants of the Abbey Mill obeyed the demand to repair its wall and bridge.

Local gentry were also involved in civic affairs both as J.P.'s and members of Parliament. Between 1571 and 1640 23 out of the 33 Cirencester M.P.'s lived in or near the town and came from families such as the Masters, the Georges of Baunton or the Pooles of Sapperton. This trend was reversed in 1645 when two well known Parliamentarians, Sir Thomas Fairfax and Nathaniel Rich represented the borough but old traditions were resumed in 1660, when Thomas Master and Henry Powle of Williamstrip Park (later Speaker of the House of Commons) were elected. Among others who sat for the borough was Sir Robert Atkyns, the historian of Gloucestershire.

By the second half of the century the wool trade had

recovered. Wills and inventories show that some Cirencester clothiers were extremely wealthy. Edward King who died in 1692 and John Cripps who died three years later left goods and possessions worth £1,100 and £1,251 respectively. Examples of the fine stone buildings in which such men lived can still be seen. In Coxwell Street beside the more imposing houses are some of the weavers' and woolcombers' cottages. Sheppard's Place in Gloucester Street, bearing the date 1694, is a reminder of similar alleyways and courtyards in which many of the poorer section of the population once lived.

The last years of the seventeenth century again brought troops to Cirencester's streets. Within three years of his accession James II's pro-Catholic policies had alienated many of his subjects and William of Orange landed at Torbay to defend the Protestant cause. The Duke of Beaufort dispatched a force to Cirencester under Captain Lorenge to intercept some of William's supporters led by Lord Lovelace. In the ensuing action Lovelace was captured, Captain Lorenge and his son killed. Another casualty was one Bulstrode Whitelocke, who died in the King's Head which today had suites of rooms named after both Whitelocke and Lovelace.

The settlement hammered out in 1689 after the so called 'Glorious Revolution' ensured a parliamentary monarchy. In future Englishmen would be more likely to seek power through political influence and patronage than force of arms. In the next century landowners would concentrate on extending and improving their estates, the middle class entrepreneurs on acquiring them. Such attitudes would be reflected in Cirencester and it is not without significance that at the very end of the seventeenth century, in 1695 the Oakley property was purchased by Sir Benjamin Bathurst, thus beginning the long connection of his family with the town and neighbourhood.

• Coxwell Street – a number of seventeenth century houses. No. 10, dated 1640 with initials I.P., was the home of John Plot, the lawyer who lived here during the Civil War. Nos. 1 and 2 are dated, respectively, 1658 and 1676. 'Woolgatherers', formerly Coxwell Court, had an adjacent warehouse which can be seen around the corner in Thomas Street. Opposite 'Woolgatherers' are former weavers' stone gabled cottages.

• Gloucester House, Dyer Street (the home of Rebecca Powell in the eighteenth century).

• No. 2 Watermoor Road – on the corner with Querns Lane (reputedly the site of the former manor house of Chesterton).

• Other seventeenth century houses survive – for details consult Verey, D. *Gloucestershire : The Cotswolds* 1979 (Cirencester perambulation) and *Cirencester – a Town Walk* published by Cirencester Civic Society.

Cirencester in the Eighteenth Century
Widening Horizons

'A very good town, populous and rich, full of clothiers and driving a great trade in wool. . . . They talk of 5,000 packs a year'. Daniel Defoe's description of Cirencester, published in his 'Tour Through England' in 1724 suggests that in the early years of the eighteenth century Cirencester's economy was dominated, as it had been since medieval times, by the wool trade. But times were changing. Another contemporary writer, Samuel Rudder in his 'History of Cirencester' in 1800 comments on the decline of the wool trade – the streets no longer blocked by great wool waggons and the rooms at the Boothall, once piled high with fleeces, now lying empty. He blamed the dealers who now preferred to buy wool direct from the farmer. Some Gloucestershire clothiers even began to travel to the great wool fairs at Dresden and Breslau, again cutting out the middleman – the wool stapler. Nevertheless a Directory of 1784 shows that Cirencester with Tetbury still shared the bulk of the wool trade in Gloucestershire – out of forty-five staplers listed, fourteen were in Cirencester and eighteen in Tetbury.

The wool trade had probably always been of greater significance to the town than the actual manufacture of cloth and now the lack of the fast water power necessary to drive the heavy fulling machines such as those of the Stroud valley ensured the latter's supremacy. Seventy clothiers are listed in the 1784 Directory – of these fifty-four were operating in the Stroud area and none are mentioned in Cirencester. Some cloth, however, continued to be produced – particularly at New Mills – 'the goodly clothing mills' built by the last Abbot. In 1780 the lease of New Mills was transferred from the Selfe family to Joseph Cripps. Here on the pasture land called 'Rack Close' the cloth would have been stretched to dry on tenter-hooks. It was at this stage that thefts sometimes occurred. In 1775 on two occasions the Gloucester Journal reported cloth stolen from New Mills –

about 'Eleven Yards of Eight Quarter Bath Coating, cut and stolen out of the tenters' and 'Fourteen Yards of White List Coarse Cloth' disappeared in the same way.

Although the Friday wool market declined the Monday corn market continued to attract farmers and dealers from a wide area. Until about 1770 England was still a corn exporting country and poor harvests could result in high grain prices. A series of disturbances in 1766 was triggered off by rumours that prices were being manipulated by farmers and bakers. Reports in the Worcester Journal speak of mills in the neighbourhood of Gloucester and Cirencester being destroyed and damage done by a large mob on market day in Cirencester who 'compelled farmers and cheese factors to sell goods at prices they themselves thought proper'. Some contemporaries thought that the problem in Cirencester was exacerbated by the change from a 'pitched' to a 'sample' market. Formerly large quantities of grain had been brought to market, now farmers carried only samples of their crops – if they liked the prices offered they sold, if not they could return home without the bother of removing grain in bulk. Rudder refers also to the old 'Assize of Bread' being no longer observed. This had allowed ordinary customers to buy small quantities of grain before farmers and dealers. In the latter part of the eighteenth century conditions further deteriorated because wages lagged behind the soaring cost of food and because of the outbreak of war with France. The years 1793–5, described by Rudder as 'the Great Dearth', were particularly distressing when 'buyers were necessitated to hunt for samples of wheat and flour and to solicit the price as a favour'.

Much of Cirencester's prosperity depended on its dealings with the inhabitants of neighbouring towns and villages. These were well served by the available commercial and professional facilities. Contemporary directories list a range of shopkeepers and the weekly markets must also have been tempting with dairy produce, beef, mutton, pork and veal as good, it was said, as any to be found in London. There was Severn salmon in season at 6d per pound and oysters from London. The town boasted four surgeons, six attorneys, several boarding schools and a dancing master. Two banks were established to support the trading community. Pitt, Bowly and Croome's Bank occupied Castle House, the fine town house in Castle Street built at the beginning of the century for a wool merchant which today is the home of Lloyds Bank. Cripp's Bank began in Coxwell Street and re-

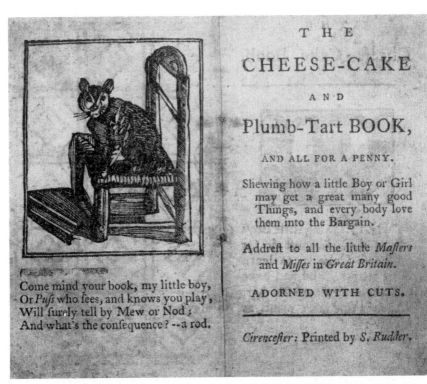

THE

CHEESE-CAKE

AND

Plumb-Tart BOOK,

AND ALL FOR A PENNY.

Shewing how a little Boy or Girl
may get a great many good
Things, and every body love
them into the Bargain.

Addreſt to all the little *Maſters*
and *Miſſes* in *Great Britain*.

ADORNED WITH CUTS.

Cirenceſter: Printed by *S. Rudder.*

Come mind your book, my little boy,
Or *Puſs* who ſees, and knows you play,
Will ſurely tell by Mew or Nod;
And what's the conſequence? --a rod.

The Cheese-Cake and Plumb Tart – a chapbook for children, published by Samuel Rudder. Back and front cover. *Courtesy Bingham Library.*

mained there until some time after 1835 when it moved to Gosditch Street to the house still known as the old Bank House.

Market days would have seen the Market Place and the surrounding streets full of jostling crowds – providing opportunities for less law abiding folk such as thieves and pickpockets. In 1744 for example the Cirencester Flying Post reported thefts from stall holders selling ribbon and lace and of a lady's handbag containing a guinea and some silver. The shops as well as the stalls would have profited from increased trade. No doubt Samuel Rudder's own shop in Dyer Street would also have been busy – here he sold not only books but also items such as cloth, tea and Sheffield ware. A copy of his 'History of Cirencester' would have cost six shillings if half bound but some of his customers would have been more interested in his cheap chapbooks, whose titles such as 'Dreadful News from Cumberland'

WHEREAS, on the 25th of this Inſtant *October*, the Houſe of *James Millington*, who keeps the *Bowling-Green*, in the Pariſh of *Cirenceſter*, was robb'd of a conſiderable Sum of Money, and ſeveral Things of Value, whoever will diſcover any of the Perſons concern'd in the ſaid Robbery, will be by Law entitled to a Reward of 40 Pounds.——There were three Perſons concern'd: One was a black full fac'd Man, with ſtrait Hair, about 5 Feet 4 Inches high, freſh colour'd; and had on brown Cloaths. Another was about 4 Feet and an half high, wore his own Hair, and had on a Linnen Frock. And the other Man was about 5 Feet and an half high, had Short Hair, with a Cap over it, and wore a light drab-colour'd Coat. They were all ſuppos'd to be about the Age of between twenty and thirty.

They took away with them in Money, &c. to the Value of 30 Pounds, among which were two Three-pound twelve Portugal Pieces, two crooked half Guineas, a French Crown Piece, and eight Queen Anne's Half Crowns; likewiſe two Gold Rings, and two Ston'd ones; as alſo a light colour'd great Coat, with remarkable long Botton Holes, which are rang'd quite down to the Bottom of the Coat; and a Gun, with a black Barrel, 5 Feet all but an Inch long, with an half Stock, and a black old-faſhion'd Lock.

October 17, 1743.

WHEREAS the Houſe of Mr. *Ralph Willett*, Rector of *Stratton*, was broke open in the Night between the 10th and 11th of this Inſtant, about Mid-night, *This is to certify*, That if any Perſon will give ſuch Information, ſo as he, ſhe, or they may be con-victed of the ſaid *Burglary*, ſuch Perſon ſhall have *Twenty Guineas* Reward immediately pay'd upon ſuch Conviction, by me

RALPH WILLETT.

* *Note*, If three Perſons were concern'd in the ſaid Fact, and one of them ſhou'd diſcover the other Two, he will be intitled to a Pardon, and *Forty Pounds* from the Government, with other Advantages, beſides the *Twenty Guineas* promiſed above.

An extract from the Cirencester Flying Post, October 1743.

Courtesy Bingham Library.

91

and 'Tippling Sal' held promise of enlivening dark winter evenings.

There were other printers and booksellers in the town. One, Thomas Hinton is said to have brought out the first number of the weekly Cirencester Flying Post in October 1718. This was one of the earliest local newspapers in the country and survived probably until early in 1724 when it succumbed to the aggressive competition of the Gloucester Journal. In the 1740's George Hill, followed by Thomas Hill, published 'The Cirencester Flying Post and Miscellany', also a weekly paper. At 1½d this was good value although more expensive as a proportion of weekly income than today. In the eighteenth century newspapers could be rented or borrowed at taverns and barbers. Mostly the news carried was national but the few local items included suggest that the Flying Post had a fairly wide circulation. Another well known bookseller was Timothy Stevens. In business in premises next to the King's Head from 1768–1802, he then went into partnership with Philip Watkins who carried on alone after Steven's death in 1816. Four volumes of the accounts of the business survive, providing not only a fascinating insight into the reading habits of the well-to-do, but also of the range of goods stocked. These included vermin killer, patent medicines, wall paper and rope as well as stationery and sheet music. The accounts contain many references to goods sent and received by carrier and coach. Stevens bought paper from Quenington and Kidderminster, pencils and art supplies from Middleton of Picadilly and Messrs. Rowney and his books from numerous London sellers. Many of his clients were not local – a Mr. Sigmond, for example, a dentist in Bath, purchased toothbrushes and toothpaste on a sale or return basis.

Cirencester traders like Stevens relied heavily on road transport. Travel had many hazards – there were dangers from highwaymen and an incident such as that reported in 1743, when Mr. Greyhurst of Cirencester was robbed between Farmington and Burford of fifty shillings and a silver watch, was not unusual. Another problem was that in winter some roads were impassable and even in good weather their surface left much to be desired. One of the worst roads was the fourteen mile stretch between Cirencester and Lechlade – the route to London via Fairford, crossing the Thames at St. John's Bridge. This was dealt with by a private Act of Parliament in 1727 which set up a Turnpike Trust. A group of local men contributed money,

An advertisement for the Ram Inn, incorporating the drawing, allegedly by William Hogarth. *Courtesy Bingham Library.*

repaired the road and then set up gates to collect tolls from users. By the end of the eighteenth century, Cirencester was the centre of a network of seven turnpiked roads. Two went to London – one via Fairford, Lechlade and Abingdon, the other through Burford and Oxford. Others maintained the town's links through surrounding counties to the Midlands and Wales. The journey to London, which in Rudder's memory, could take three days, could now be accomplished in summer in one day in the Cirencester 'Flying Machine'. Regular services were advertised such as the 'True Briton' from the Crown to London on Sundays, Wednesdays and Fridays at 6.00 am and the 'Safety Briton' from the Ram on Tuesdays, Thursdays and Saturdays at 7.00 am. Inside travelling was for the wealthy as the fare was twenty-eight shillings, with half this sum for the more uncomfortable outside. This was the heyday of the coaching inns, for example the Ram in Castle Street with its entrance in the Market Place and the King's Head with its capacious stable accommodation. Local business records contain references to carriers such as Masters and Niblett who were obviously used with great trust by their patrons. When George Cumberland, brother of the Rector of Driffield, lost his dog in Abergavenny he gave instructions that if the animal were found, he should be sent home by the waggon which went through Cirencester from Abergavenny every Sunday evening. On another occasion one of the Cumberlands' relatives sent by coach from London a cask of Jamaican rum to be left at the Ram for collection.

From 1741 there was a daily postal service between London and Bristol, the route running through Oxford, Cirencester and Gloucester. From 1781 the mail was carried by mailcoach although occasionally bad conditions prevented this from getting through. In January 1795 the Superintendent of Mail Coaches reported that 'John Jeffs rode all the way from Cirencester to Oxford and back through snow and water, the coach not being able to proceed either way. He was not wetted but through great exertion was on time with his mail'.

Despite the improvements in the roads, it was still difficult and costly to convey heavy goods by land. The completion of the Stroudwater Canal in 1779 enabled the Severn River trade to work up to Stroud and interest revived in a link between the Severn and the Thames. Following a public meeting backed by Earl Bathurst in 1781, the route was surveyed by Robert Whitworth, a pupil of James Brindley. The initial estimated cost of £128,000 was raised and by 1789 the 29 mile long canal was finished, the major engineering problem having been the famous Sapperton Tunnel. Cirencester was the terminus of a branch of this canal, just over a mile in length, connecting with the main route at Siddington. The Cirencester Basin was situated between Querns Hill and Workhouse Lane (now Querns Road) in the triangular area now filled in. Here there were three wharves and a wharfhouse – the latter survived until 1975. When the first coal barges arrived in May 1789 a great crowd turned out to watch. The link with the Thames at Lechlade was completed in November of the same year. The main inward traffic was coal but other goods such as salt, bricks, slate and timber came into Cirencester. The bulk of the outward traffic was in grain.

The canal aroused royal interest also. In 1788 George III and Queen Charlotte with three of the royal Princesses, visited Cirencester Park on their way to take the waters at Cheltenham. As well as the Park, they saw the nearly completed Sapperton

Allen Bathurst, 1st Baronet.   *Courtesy Bingham Library.*

Tunnel, expressing 'most decided astonishment at the work of such magnitude, expense and general utility'. They were also more than delighted with the 'woods, groves and gardens' of the Park itself. Cirencester Park owed its existence to the inspiration of the 1st. Earl Bathurst. He had inherited the Oakley Estate from his father, Sir Benjamin Bathurst in 1704, at the age of twenty. In the same year he married his cousin, the sixteen year old Catherine Apsley and in 1705 was elected as one of Cirencester's M.Ps. in the Tory interest. He won the favour of Queen Anne who visited Oakley Grove in 1708 and raised him to the peerage

Oakley House – two views from Samuel Rudder's History of Cirencester.

View of Cirencester, drawn by John Kyp, c. 1712.   *Courtesy Bingham Library.*

in 1712. The death of his patroness and the accession of George I, who favoured the Whigs, caused Lord Bathurst to withdraw from the political scene and devote more time to his estate. He purchased the rest of Oakley woods and the manor of Sapperton from the Atkyns family and the Barton estate from Sir Richard Onslow. He then proceeded to develop his country seat on the edge of the town, unlike many of his contemporaries who isolated themselves from their neighbours, sometimes removing whole villages in the process. The Kyp engraving of Oakley Grove in Sir Robert Atkyns 'History of Gloucestershire' published in 1712 shows the house as an E–shaped structure with gables and end wings. Soon after, this was demolished and replaced by a rectangular building, not especially new in style.

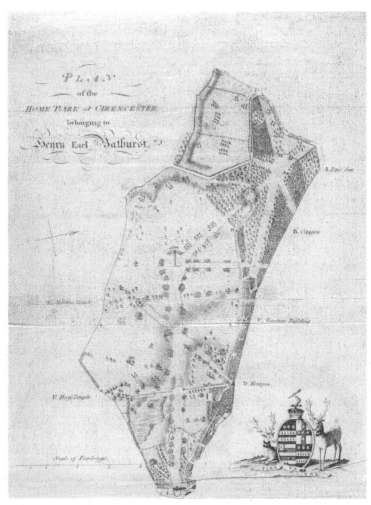

Plan of Cirencester Park (1), Rudder, History of Cirencester

Lord Bathurst, probably his own architect, was reported not to have been particularly pleased with the result, asking 'How comes it to look so oddly bad?'.

In landscaping the Park, however, Lord Bathurst was supremely confident and successful. In his plans he was aided and encouraged by the poet Alexander Pope who was one of a circle of some of the foremost intellects of the day such as Dean Swift, Thomas Gay and Lawrence Sterne, who surrounded Lord Bath-

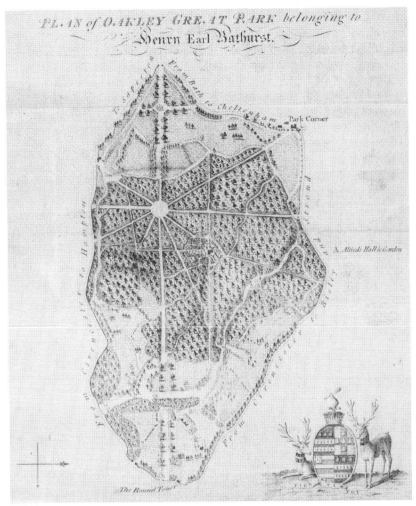

Plan of Cirencester Park (2), Rudder, History of Cirencester.

urst, attracted by his wit and generosity. The Park was laid out 'to create the aimiable simplicity of unadorned nature' although some contemporaries commented on its formal French air.. An expert in forestry Lord Bathurst made woods and glades in hitherto open country, adding interest with buildings and follies. Some of these like the Hexagon and Pope's Seat were in the classical tradition, others like the Round House and Ivy House were precursors of the Neo-Gothic revival. The Woodhouse or

Alfred's Hall is today considered especially important as the earliest of all the castellated follies. Vistas or rides were constructed, the most famous being the Broad Ride which stretches from the Park Gates on Cecily Hill to the Golden Valley at Sapperton.

In 1775, three years after he had been created Earl, Lord Bathurst died in his ninety-first year 'regretted by most and praised by all' according to his epitaph in the Parish Church. His eldest surviving son, Henry, inherited his estate. The second Earl Bathurst had made his career at the Bar, rising to the office of Lord Chancellor in 1771. He continued his father's landscaping projects although it was not until 1814, in the time of the third Earl that the old Stroud road which ran up Cecily Hill and crossed the main drive to emerge at Park Corner, was closed. The third Earl then constructed the present more direct road running from the junction of the old Tetbury Road, along the back of the Agricultural College and down Kill Devil Hill.

The other leading family in the town was that of the Masters. In December 1742 Thomas Master married Elizabeth Chester Cann, heiress of her father, Sir William Cann and niece of Thomas Chester of Knole Park, Almondsbury, 'a beautiful young lady with a Fortune upwards of £30,000'. The couple took up residence in the Elizabethan manor built on the site of the former Abbey but in 1776 this was demolished to make way for the house which survived until the 1960's.

For most of the eighteenth century the Bathursts and the Masters shared the control of the two Parliamentary seats, despite the fact that, for the period, Cirencester, a 'pot walloper' borough, had a comparatively large electorate of about six hundred made up of male householders of at least six months duration and not receiving alms. Usually the nominees of the Bathursts and Masters were returned unopposed – if there were other candidates they were defeated as in 1722 and 1727. In 1762 Lord Bathurst wrote to his friend, the Reverend Joshua Parry, Presbyterian minister in the town, that if his nominee were not accepted 'it would be time for me to find another place of residence'. However, in the election of 1754 events did not follow the usual pattern. Canvassing started early – in the previous year – a sign of the excitement engendered. Henry Bathurst and John Coxe (supported by the Masters) were seeking re-election but rumour spread that Henry's elder brother, Benjamin, was also proposing to stand. Opposition against the possibility of the Bathursts controlling both seats mounted, and when Henry Bathurst and his supporters entered the town in 1753, they were attacked by Masters' followers, known as the 'We's' as they passed the gate of Abbey House en route to the Market Place. The horses, frightened by handbells, threw many of their riders who were attacked with dirt and stones. There were other violent scenes and at least one Bathurst supporter, Tom Jordan, was killed. He was commemorated in a specially written ballad by Joshua Parry. In the end both Henry Bathurst and John Coxe retired and Benjamin Bathurst and John Dawney, a newcomer, were elected.

Violence also erupted at several other elections. In 1768 supporters of Samuel Blackwell clashed with those of James Whiteshed at the Ram, and there was evidence of attempts to influence voters and to swell the electorate by bringing in outsiders as temporary residents. Part of the opposition came from wealthy entrepreneurs like the Cripps who, having achieved economic status, now had political aspirations. Able to command support in the town as bankers, brewers and clothiers, their influence was further strengthened by marriage links with other leading families such as the Selfes and the Lawrences and indirectly, the Bowlys. The Cripps did not directly contest an election until 1806 but in 1790 Robert Preston, a wealthy ship owner and naval commander in the East India Company, ousted Richard Master after a petition to the House of Commons.

Other controversies disturbed the equilibrium of Cirencester's citizens. A dispute over the mastership of the Grammar School in 1754 between Henry Wightwick and Francis James aroused much feeling. As a result of the ensuing law suit the right of appointment was taken out of local control and vested in the Lord Chancellor. One of the school's most famous pupils, Edward Jenner, the pioneer of vaccination against small pox was in attendance around this time. However, under Dr. Washbourne, headmaster for most of the second half of the century, numbers declined until, in 1783, he is said to have dismissed the school's one remaining pupil and returned to Oxford, though still continuing to draw his salary!

There was trouble too between the Reverend Samuel Johnson, who replaced Joseph Harrison as minister of the parish church in 1753, and his parishioners. In 1775 they quarrelled over the election of a new parish clerk. Timothy Stevens, the bookseller,

Gloucester House, Dyer Street. *Photo. A. Welsford.*

was elected at the vestry meeting but Johnson appointed an attorney, Thomas Lediard. Eventually Stevens was accepted but only after some unpleasant incidents, including being locked out of the church. Samuel Johnson had long enjoyed the Bathurst favour but after the death of the 1st Earl this diminished and in 1778 he agreed to accept a new living in Sussex.

Possibly some of his parishioners found his friendly relations with the Bathursts unpalatable and some may also have found his vigorous and enthusiastic preaching style unacceptable. Such methods were probably considered more the province of the Dissenters who certainly in the early decades of the century were a fairly large body. According to Archbishop Benson's survey in 1735 they numbered some seven hundred, about 18% of the total population. Other evidence suggests some decline after this but many well-to-do and influential people were connected with this group, such as Francis Hoare, the woolstapler who was a Baptist, and members of the Bowly and the Wilkins families who were Quakers. The Presbyterians were also well connected – the daughter of woolstapler, Caleb Hillier, married their minister, Joshua Parry who was himself well known in literary circles and a friend of the first Earl Bathurst.

The eighteenth century Evangelical movement was perhaps

102

best represented by the Methodists. George Whitfield visited Cirencester in 1739, preaching in the amphitheatre as he had been refused use of the parish church. John Wesley made a number of visits – in 1750 he preached to 'a large but not serious congregation' but in 1787, in the Weavers' Hall 'they all drank in the Word as the thirsty earth the showers'. There appear to be no records of the actual founding of Cirencester Methodist Church but the Weslyan Methodist building in Gloucester Street was erected in 1808 for 300 people.

The interior of the parish church was altered during this period. Box pews were erected for wealthy families to rent and galleries were constructed, blocking entrances to some of the chapels and part of the west window. The maintenance of the church was the responsibility of the churchwardens and their accounts contain items such as the payment of £14-5s to John Flux for repainting the altar and the royal arms and regilding and painting the two dials and weathercock on the tower. An almost annual expense was the payment for sweeping snow from the church roof.

The churchwardens together with the overseers of the poor were also involved in the collection and expenditure of the parish poor rate. In 1724 Lord Bathurst gave a house at Chesterton for use as a workhouse, and Gabriel Cook was appointed Master at an annual salary of £50. Every effort was made to keep 'outdoor' relief to a minimum and to control losses by setting the poor to work. Even so, in 1778 the poor law account was so much in arrears that £400 had to be borrowed to meet current expenses. Sometimes paupers, wearing their brown coats and distinctive badges, were hired out to local clothiers but the only known example of 'farming out' the administration, common elsewhere, occurs in 1780 when Joseph Cripps offered to maintain all the poor, inside and outside the workhouse for not more that £1,100 a year.

The health of the poor was a matter of concern – chiefly as a precaution against the spread of epidemics like smallpox. In 1732 a building described as adjoining the Querns and in the possession of Richard Gegg was leased from Lord Bathurst for £5 per annum as a pesthouse and contracts with local apothecaries to act as medical officers of health appear from 1738. The annual salary of £10 increased to £30 by 1800. In 1796 the town's apothecaries agreed that they would not innoculate any persons unless they remained in the pesthouse until free of infection.

Several weeks later they agreed to stop all innoculation for the next six months except where absolutely necessary.

The poor were helped by wealthy and conscientious philanthropists, and the town was also well endowed from previous centuries. Amongst the numerous benefactors were Mrs. Elizabeth Cripps and her sister, Miss Clutterbuck who left an annual sum for 10 widows or unmarried women, not otherwise receiving relief, and John Day who left land to provide for 'poor, decayed housekeepers' in Cirencester and Minchinhampton. The most significant charitable institutions of this period were the Blue and Yellow Schools. The Blue School, endowed originally by Thomas Powell to supplement money given by local inhabitants, opened in 1714 in a house in Gloucester Street, to give a basic Christian education to twenty boys and twenty girls. The Yellow School in 1722, was endowed under the will of Thomas Powell's widow, Rebecca, a very wealthy and much married lady. Because of a legal dispute this School, also in Gloucester Street, did not open until 1740. It catered for forty boys and twenty girls who were clothed and educated. The boys were also taught the craft of stocking weaving and the girls were taught to spin.

Unfortunately the attempt to establish stocking weaving in the town by this means was unsuccessful, but there were other positive efforts to help poor boys acquire useful skills. The Cirencester Society in London founded towards the end of the seventeenth century had as one of its objectives, the apprenticing of poor Cirencester boys. According to its records at least ninety-one boys were thus helped in the eighteenth century, among them familiar names such as Gilman and Radway.

The legal endorsement of apprenticeship agreements was one of the many responsibilities of the local J.P.s Drawn from the propertied classes, their judgements often reflected a fear of disorder and the harsh laws of the day were strictly enforced. In 1766, for example, three men were transported for stealing flour and meal from a Mr. Norris. There was, of course, more serious crime to be dealt with – in 1743 James Millington's house at the Bowling Green was broken into by three men, he was wounded and his wife fatally stabbed. The men were apprehended – two were sent to Gloucester Gaol and the third Thomas Teptoe, detained in Cirencester Bridewell (which was next to the Bear Inn) to await the next Assize. A spate of burglaries in 1790 caused a number of citizens to form a 'Bond of Association'

The original Yellow School Building, Gloucester Street, now part of Powell's School.   *Photo. A. Welsford.*

The bust of Rebecca Powell in Cirencester Parish Church.
Courtesy Miss J. Barker.

pledged to prosecute at their own expense 'all persons who shall dare to commit any kind of theft or violence on the properties of the associates'. Rewards for the apprehension and conviction of offenders ranged from £10-10-0d for burglary and arson to £2-2-0d for sheep stealing and robbing orchards or gardens.

The excesses of the French Revolution and the outbreak of war with France in 1793 intensified the fears of the upper and middle classes, although an invitation in 1792 for voluntary contributions to defend the constitution raised only £4-14-0d from which £3-17-0d had to be taken for expenses. Later enterprises were more successful. The Cirencester Volunteer Corps founded in 1798, was pledged to prevent and suppress tumult and riot. Members paraded weekly under their captain, Joseph Cripps, in uniforms of his own design.

For the more leisured, life in the eighteenth century was not unpleasant. Visits could be made to Assemblies in the Great Room of the Bell Inn or to plays performed in the yard of The Three Cocks in Castle Street or Cirencester Theatre later adapted as the Loyal Volunteer in Gloucester Street. In the latter actors and actresses of national repute, including Sarah Siddons, appeared. There were the famous Woodhouse concerts in Cirencester Park and in summer also race meetings at Cerney Down on the Whiteway or Tetbury or further afield in Bibury. Cricket was played – the Gloucester Journal of 1769 recorded that 'the young gentlemen of Cirencester are introducing the manly exercise of cricket into this county'. Cock fighting is also recorded at the King's Head in 1767 and other wagers were made at the Bull Club which met usually at the Old Bull Inn in Dyer Street and numbered among its members prominent men in the town.

Another club meeting in Cirencester was intended to promote more intellectual pursuits. This was the Book Club founded by the Reverend Richard Cumberland and based at the premises of Timothy Stevens. Twelve members each paid a monthly subscription of one shilling. Books were purchased by common agreement and at the end of the year sold to members at an auction. Local clergymen and business and professional men made up the group and their dominant interests of contemporary conditions and political issues revealed in their purchases show that they were by no means unaware of the great social and economic changes which were taking place or of current events and ideas.

Plan of Cirencester 1795 by Richard Hall.   *Courtesy Bingham Library.*

WHAT TO SEE

● Cirencester Park – open to visitors on foot by kind permission of Earl Bathurst. Entrances in Cecily Hill and the Tetbury Road.

● Lloyd's Bank, Castle Street, once the home of a wealthy wool-merchant – 'the best example of Palladian architecture in Cirencester' (Verey).

● Yellow School Building, Gloucester Street – now handsomely restored as part of Powell's School.

● There are eighteenth century houses in many of the main streets – particularly Cecily Hill, Coxwell Street, Dollar Street, Gloucester Street, Park Street and Thomas Street. For details consult Verey, D., *Gloucestershire The Cotswolds* 1979 (Cirencester perambulation) and *Cirencester – a Town Walk* published by Cirencester Civic Society.

Cirencester in the Early Nineteenth Century
Hard Times and Improvements

An inhabitant of the town in 1800 would have detected little outward change in its appearance from the previous century. Circumscribed by the Bathurst and Abbey estates, its life and business were carried on in the narrow streets radiating from the congested Market Place. Links with the surrounding countryside were still strong – the 1811 census returns show nearly a quarter of the families engaged in agriculture. People kept pigs in their backyards and there were market gardens and nurseries within walking distance of the Market Place itself.

However, the changing structure of agriculture and industry, fluctuations in wage levels and rising inflation would inevitably have had an impact on this small community of some 4,000 people. Evidence from surviving poll books suggests that increased mechanisation was affecting the pattern of employment in the town. In 1790 just over 13% of the 600 male householders eligible to vote were employed in textile manufacture. By 1812 this had fallen to 9%. The once thriving craft of wool combing was also in decline – the 34 combers named in 1790 have dwindled to 17 by 1812. Neither are there any Cirencester names among the 78 Gloucestershire manufacturers who met in 1802 to campaign for the repeal of obsolete statutes governing the woollen industry. Several leading families like the Budds and the Hoares, however, continued to be associated with the wool sorting business until well on into the nineteenth century. Today Coxwell Street with its former wool-workers' cottages and grander houses of the clothiers in close proximity is a reminder of the once great era of Cirencester wool.

Two mills continued to operate for some time. At New Mills, 'the goodly clothing mills' mentioned by Leland, Joseph Cripps junior produced a worsted cloth called 'thin stuff' or 'chinas', used mainly for servants' dresses. In its undyed state it was exported by the East India Company. Cloth manufacture ceased

110

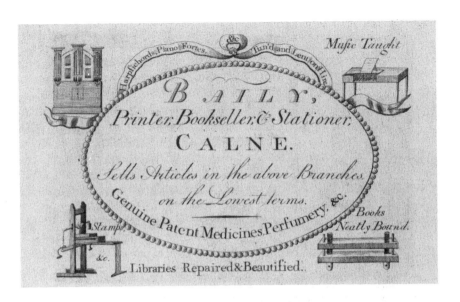

Shop and Trade Card of T.P. Baily who took over the business of Philip Watkins.   *Courtesy Bingham Library.*

here in the early years of the nineteenth century. The Cripps' other mill at Stratton operated until 1842. In 1839 a government report on the Condition of the Handloom Weavers stated that 'Messrs. Cripps have a small factory – the work is all put out to be woven – price £1 per piece and all is conducted in the human feeling of giving work to the poor rather than for profit'.

The carpet factory in Gloucester Street run by Kendall and Bullock and then by the Silk brothers from Kidderminster, did a good trade with America as well as the home market. About 100 hands were employed and its yearly profits were around £1,000. The closure of the factory about 1839 seems to have been the result of competition from more advanced machinery.

The only other craft deemed worthy of mention by Rudder was that of edge-tool manufacture – particularly the fine curriers' knives which it was claimed found a market all over Europe and America. The number of men employed in this enterprise also declined in the nineteenth century although two family businesses, the Deightons and the Lanes, continued to operate until the second half of the century.

To contemporaries clear evidence of changing economic circumstances must have been the reduction of the weekly Friday market, once originally mainly for wool, to a market for general commodities. However, there was no shortage of farmers and dealers at the Monday corn market. Cirencester, mid way between the corn-producing counties of the north and east and the populous manufacturing areas of the south and west, was ideally situated. Its market was thought to be at least the equal of Gloucester and on market days the narrow lanes of the Market Place must have echoed to the shouts of traders and customers. Farmers with samples of grain in their wallets stood in the open, the windows of the White Hart Inn providing a convenient resting place for their wares. Inflation and bad harvests caused fluctuations in the price of grain which were particularly worrying for the poor. Governments sought to secure a protected market for the powerful agricultural interest by a series of measures which culminated in the famous Corn Laws of 1815. Even so a meeting of farmers at the Ram Inn, in 1826, condemned 'the extraordinary policy of encouraging Foreigners to the total Ruin of the home trade'.

Local initiative was still expected to provide help to the poor and needy. In 1800 the well-to-do in Cirencester were urged to cut their bread consumption by one third to ensure adequate

The Bowly Almshouses, Watermoor Road.   *Photo. A. Welsford.*

supplies for the poor and £600 was raised for the 'industrious poor'. The great age of the charity trusts had almost passed but in 1803 a trust was set up for the 'Benefit of Poor Lying-in Women' to provide them with the services of a mid-wife and a yard and a half of flannel. Gloucestershire magistrates adopted the Speenhamland system of supplementing wages from the poor rate, based on the price of the bread a family was thought to need for survival. Money from the rate was also used to support those unable to work. They would either be given outdoor relief (a money payment allowing them to remain in their own homes) or sent to the poor house. In 1801 – a record year – nearly £4,000 was raised by the parish of Cirencester of which over £3,000 was spent. A very small amount of this would have been offset by the work done by the occupants of the poor house but the rising costs of supporting the impoverished caused much concern. It was no wonder that Cirencester, like other parishes, exercised its right to return non-parishioners to their place of birth. One such was Elizabeth Harris who, in 1812, was sent with her three children to the parish of Barton St. Mary in Gloucester where her husband had been born. He was a former Charity School orphan who had deserted her as he had been forced to travel the country looking for work.

Unsettled economic conditions must have also affected the town's traders although there might have been some mitigation in the soldiers and militia who were stationed in Cirencester or who travelled through the town. Some business accounts reveal a surprising tolerance to debt, perhaps an indication of a close-knit commercial community. When Samuel Gibbs, last of a long line of tallow chandlers in Cricklade Street, died in 1819, he was in debt to a local butcher, Edmund Young, for tallow amounting to £2,000. The account had been unpaid for many years. Samuel's bill from Richardson's, the tailors, included 2d for mending his brother Daniel's coat as a boy together with the same Daniel's funeral expenses in 1816. In turn the Gibbs were owed £69 for soap and candles, supplied to the Richardsons between 1797 and 1819.

Traders as well as the community in general were dependent on road and canal transport for maintaining contacts outside the town. Carriers like Tanner and Baylis and William Budd operated regular daily services to London, Bath, Bristol and intermediate stages while most of the nearby villages and towns had at least a weekly service. Coal and grain in particular continued to be carried by canal. In 1825 an Act of Parliament formed the Cirencester District of Roads which consolidated under one authority all the turnpike roads to the town except that to Wootton Bassett. A new road to Cheltenham was opened in 1827, branching off at Stratton at what was called the Salutation Gate and following a winding but more direct route through the Churn valley. Hitherto the main route to Cheltenham had been via the old Roman road to Gloucester, branching off at the top of the Cotswolds. Coach travel was still not entirely without hazard. In 1816 the Cirencester Gleaner reported that the London coach had set off from the Swan without a driver and had to be stopped at the turnpike beyond Dyer Street by a post chaise drawn across the road. In 1814 both Cirencester banks lost parcels of banknotes amounting to a total of nearly £5,000 which were being sent by coach to their London correspondent banks.

Notwithstanding, the bank of Pitt, Bowly and Croome, and that of Cripps were both successful according to Rudder in conducting their business 'with great regularity and prudence'. In 1802

Pitt, Bowly and Croome had amongst its securities a holding of State Lottery tickets. The State Lottery was a popular method used by the government to raise money. In 1815 the bank made a profit of just over £3,000 on buying and selling lottery tickets. The Cirencester Savings Bank was established in 1817 and although the economic climate was not particularly favourable, by the end of the year there were 144 accounts and a balance of £2,838. From its beginnngs in the Town Hall, the Bank moved in 1854 to buildings in Park Lane.

The government's call for more men to supplement the militia when hostilities were resumed against France in 1803 was answered in Cirencester by the raising of a volunteer cavalry force by Earl Bathurst. Part of their training consisted of a sham fight in Cirencester Park when the volunteers, acting as the enemy, were attacked by the militia. The battle was followed by a picnic to which ladies were invited and the militia band then accompanied the dancing. Families of men serving with the militia were the responsibility of the community. The records of the Overseers of the Poor in 1803 list thirty men whose wives were receiving assistance and similar lists appear until 1815 – in that year one man is recorded as a prisoner in France. Members of leading families in the town responded readily to government appeals – Devereux Bowly, Stephen Wilkins, Henry Zachary and Francis Hoare contributed £112–2–0d between them towards the purchase of warm woollen underwear for volunteers.

The prominence of such names in the war effort illustrates that this was a period when members of the entrepreneurial class sought and achieved economic wealth and social status. In Cirencester, as elsewhere, they also challenged other preserves of the ruling groups. The highly controversial election of 1790 encouraged others to follow the example of wealthy outsider, Robert Preston (see chapter 7). Another outsider, Thomas Bayley Howell, builder of the Tontine terrace of cottages on Cecily Hill, was unsuccessful in the elections of 1796 and 1802, but four years later a local candidate from the middle class manufactur-ing interest emerged. Joseph Cripps – whose connections with banking, brewing and cloth manufacture were likely to create a core of support among the electorate – was persuaded to stand by Joseph Pitt, a local solicitor, banker and land speculator. Suc-cessful at the 1806 election, Cripps was defeated in 1812 when the poll lasted five days and cost the candidates a great deal of money. One of Cripps' opponents spent £12,000 and many

The Tontine Building, Cecily Hill.   *Photo. A. Welsford.*

electors took advantage of the 2s 6d and 5s 0d tickets given for refreshment at local inns. Joseph Cripps however was victorious in 1818 and remained as M.P. until he resigned in 1841.

For some of the poorer sections of the community, elections must have been a welcome diversion as well as potentially lucrative. Seasonal entertainments like the annual Mop or hiring fair were also an eagerly awaited relaxation – even the paupers in the workhouse were sometimes given a small sum to spend on these occasions. At other times the poor probably frequented one of the numerous public houses. A list in the Gloucestershire Record Office from about 1800, names seventy-three public houses, forty-one of which are noted as having been recently suppressed. Some of these have picturesque names such as the Pot of the Four Combers in Dollar Ward and the Three Cats' Heads in St. Lawrence Ward.

Like many towns, Cirencester celebrated prematurely the downfall of Napoleon in 1814. Napoleon's return to France from Elba enabled one Cirencester citizen to fulfil an ambition. At the beginning of 1815 Charles Lawrence and a friend visited Paris in order to see the French Emperor and managed to get a front seat at Napoleon's review of 60,000 French troops. Charles wrote to his fiancee, Lydia Bowly, giving her his impressions. No doubt on his return Charles Lawrence was a popular visitor at many a

116

The Lock up – once at the end of Gloucester Street, now in the grounds of Cotswold District Council Offices, Watermoor. *Photo. A. Welsford.*

Cirencester home. In 1816 another welcome visitor was the hero of Waterloo himself, the Duke of Wellington, who passed through on his way to Longleat. Some of the cheering crowds were allowed on to the lawns of the Mansion to shake his hand. The Duke was occasionally a guest at Cirencester having formed a firm friendship with the third Earl Bathurst who as Secretary for War and the Colonies had supported his campaigns.

The ending of the war brought returning soldiers to swell an already overfull labour market and adjustments to a peace-time economy were painful. Although not specifically affected by disturbances taking place elsewhere, there were undoubtedly wild and unruly elements among Cirencester's population. A correspondent in the 'Gleaner' in 1816 referred to the 'nightly Assembly of many disorderly men and boys outside the Ram Inn' whose 'continual noisy rioting precludes all possibility of rest'. Isolated incidents also indicate a potentially explosive situation. In 1825 when William Taylor knocked down a soldier and was taken to the lock-up, a large crowd of some 200 threw stones. However, during the Swing riots of 1830, involving destruction of agricultural machinery in places not far from the town, 129

117

townspeople signed their willingness to be sworn in as special constables. It was in Cirencester that the magistrates issued in 1831 'An Appeal to the Peasantry' warning the rioters that military force would be used against them.

Having failed at an earlier period to achieve borough status, the town continued to be governed under the dual system of the manorial jurisdiction now vested in the Bathurst family and of the parish in conjunction with the local Justices of the Peace who from Elizabethan times had everywhere been increasingly burdened with administrative responsibilities. By the early nineteenth century these arrangements were generally inadequate to cope with all the increasingly complex social and economic problems and in many areas ad hoc bodies such as the Turnpike Trusts and Improvement Commissioners were set up. In 1825 Cirencester gained its own Improvement Commission by a private act of Parliament. The Act allowed for the sale of common land at Watermoor and Kingsmead to provide money for the changes to be brought about. Compensation would be given to those with common grazing rights. Some indication of what was needed is given in the pre-amble to the Act 'whereas the town of Cirencester is large and populous, the footpaths in several of the streets and lanes and public passages are not sufficiently repaired, cleansed, drained, lighted and watched, are subject to various obstructions and are unsafe for passengers and travellers . . .'.

The terms of the Act were numerous and specific. The hundred men named as Commissioners were empowered to raise an annual rate not exceeding 4s-6d in the pound. They had to be owners of land or property within the town worth at least £50 a year or possessed of personal estate of at least £1,500. Meetings were to be held monthly at the Town Hall, seven commissioners constituting a quorum. Throughout the fifty years of their existence usually never more than 28–30 attended meetings. Inhabitants were required, among other things, to sweep the pavement outside their houses weekly, not to remove night soil at any other times than those laid down, and not to obstruct roads and footways. They were not 'wantonly to let off or discharge any gun, pistol, blunderbuss, serpent or rocket, or throw any cracker, squib or other firework or play at football or any game or games to the annoyance of any inhabitant or passenger'. Penalties ranged from a maximum of £5 for infringing the night soil regulations to two shillings for every foot of hedge causing an

The Market Place, 1805.   *Courtesy Bingham Library.*

The Market Place about 1840.   *Courtesy Bingham Library.*

119

obstruction.

There was a flurry of activities in the first years after the Act. Two water carts were purchased and a tender accepted from Calvin Evans, scavenger. Daniel Trinder was instructed to investigate the feasibility of an effective drainage system and in 1831, William Herbert from Kidderminster was authorised to supply, light and clean 150–180 oil lamps for street lighting. This was a short term measure since in 1833, with the Commissioners' approval, William Morley Stears, a gas engineer from Leeds, designed and executed the two small gas holders which supplied the town until 1854. The Gas Works were situated on the canal bank at a sufficient distance to prevent a nuisance to the inhabitants.

The major project of these early years was of course the clearing away of the lanes, shops and houses which encumbered the middle of the Market Place. The sale of the common land raised about £5,000 and this together with the proceeds of public subscriptions was sufficient to enable the demolition and re-housing to take place. By 1830 Shoe Lane, Butter Row and Botcher Row had disappeared. The other buildings in the Market Place such as the Shambles and the old 'blind' house also went as did the houses adjoining the church porch. The wall of the porch was weakened in the process since it was honeycombed with flues which had been built into it. The Town Commissioners lent the church authorities £1,000 to assist with the reconstruction of the south porch of the church. The noise and upheaval during this period must have been considerable and probably not all approved of the changes but a near contemporary print of 1840 published by the local printer Keyworth gives some idea of how great was the transformation.

Cirencester was affected by other Acts of Parliament during this period. The 1832 Parliamentary Reform Act reduced the size of the local electorate. Hitherto all male householders of at least six months duration had been eligible to vote but the new uniform urban franchise was for occupiers of property worth £10 a year or more. The poorer sections of the population would now be unable to vote although those already enfranchised under the old system retained the right for their life-time. The boundary of the parliamentary borough was now equated with that of the parish.

The Poor Law Amendment Act of 1834 also had consequences for the town. Its aim was to end the old system of parish relief.

The Cotswold District Council Offices, formerly the Poor Law Institution.
Photo. A. Welsford.

Parishes were grouped into unions and local Boards of Guardians superseded the overseers of the poor. As far as possible 'outdoor' relief was abolished and those unable to support themselves were to be obliged to enter the workhouse. The Cirencester Union consisted of Cirencester and thirty-eight other parishes. In 1836 the site of the former parish poor house at Watermoor was purchased from Earl Bathurst for £1,038 and a workhouse building with a capacity for 300 inmates was erected, together with the lock-up for the recalcitrant, removed from Gloucester Street. Mr. and Mrs. George Lane were appointed Master and Matron at annual salaries of £40 and £20 respectively. The proposed diet, when submitted for official approval, provoked the question whether it was intended that on five days out of seven, dinner for male inmates should consist of 1lb of potatoes. In reply the local Board asserted that this was 'the usual diet of the independent labourer in the district'. Within a couple of years, however, a slightly more varied fare had been introduced. Early reports of the visiting committee show that the workhouse was not immediately fully occupied – in the first year or so only one able-bodied male was present. By the 1851 census,

Watermoor House.   *Photo. A. Welsford.*

there were 245 inmates of whom 100 were children.

Even outside the workhouse, conditions in the crowded courts and alleyways of some of the main streets were probably cramped and uncongenial, in marked contrast to larger houses being built and occupied by some of the prosperous middle classes. Watermoor House was completed by solicitor Joseph Mullings in 1827. Charles Lawrence, another solicitor, persuaded Earl Bathurst to lease him part of the Querns, opposite the entrance to Cirencester Park. Here he erected a substantial ornamental villa, now forming part of the Querns Hospital site. Charles Lawrence's father-in-law, Devereux Bowly had already built Chesterton House in 1813. Ashcroft House, situated at the junction of Cricklade Street and Querns Lane with its surrounding orchards, pleasure gardens and stables was inherited by Joseph Cripps in 1830 from his bachelor brother.

Social life for the middle class was agreable and varied. There were theatrical performances at the theatre in Gloucester Street and balls at the King's Head and the Assembly Rooms. Margaret Ann Croome, daughter of the vicar of Bourton-on-the-Water who visited her Cirencester relations in 1823 and 1829 mentions in her diary dances at which she 'returned a little before 2 a.m. and for partners did not move out of the Cripps' family'. Public concerts were not infrequent and annual attractions such as the

The Querns. *Courtesy Bingham Library.*

shows of the Agricultural and Horticultural Associations, both founded in 1829 would have afforded entertainment for some.

Others felt the need for a more serious use of leisure. An attempt in 1827 to establish a library 'for the circulation of instructive books among the mechanics and working classes' failed. Eight years later, in 1835, it was agreed to form a Public Library with a newsroom. Initially this would be funded by the sale of fifty shares at £10 each. The running costs would be met by annual subscription. Not all approved – some thought a newsroom might become a focus of political unrest. Nevertheless a house was rented in Dyer Street and Samuel Overthrow, a local book binder, was appointed Honorary Librarian. At first all went well – there were 170 subscribers in the first year and a museum was added which housed gifts such as fourteen stuffed birds from Edward Bowly, as well Roman antiquities. Early enthusiasm, however, was not maintained and already in 1838 there were references to a 'numerous class of persons who do not avail themselves of so valuable a Library'. By this time Victoria had become Queen and the fortunes of the library are part of the town's history during her long reign.

FOR THE BENEFIT OF

Mr. KNOWLES,

Box-Office-Keeper.

NEW THEATRE CIRENCESTER.

On MONDAY the 4th of JANUARY, 1802,

Will be acted SHERIDAN's favorite COMEDY

The RIVALS,

Or, A TRIP TO BATH.

THE PART OF

Acres by Mr. STANLEY,

(From the Theatres-Royal *Edinburgh, York,* and *Dublin,* his first Appearance on this STAGE.)

Faulkland, Mr. BUCKLE.——Capt. Absolute, Mr. WESTON.
Sir Lucius O'Trigger. Mr. SWINDALL.——Fag. Mr. H CHAMBERLAIN.
David, Mr. SMITH.——And Sir Anthony Absolute, Mr. CHAMBERLAIN.
Julia. Miss PARSONS.—— Mrs. Malaprop, Mrs. SMITH.
Lucy, Mrs. FIELD.——And Lydia Languish, Mrs. CARLETON.

TWO COMIC SONGS BETWEEN THE ACTS.

After which will be perform'd a humorous INTERLUDE, call'd

The GHOST;

Or, The affrighted FARMER.

Captain Constant. Mr. *Buckle.*——Sir Jeffrey, Mr. *Smith.*
Trusty, Mr. *Chamberlain*—Clinch. Mr. *H. Chamberlain.*
And Roger, Mr *Richards.*

Belinda, Miss *Weston.*——And Dorothy, Mrs. *Field.*

Singing between the Acts, by Miss WESTON and Miss WALTON.

To which will be added, The popular FARCE of

My Grandmother.

Dicky Gossip, (with the Song on all Trades) Mr. *Richards.*
Sir Matthew Medley. Mr. *Smith.*——Woodley, Mr. *Weston.*
Souffrance, Mr. *H. Chamberlain.*——And Vapour, Mr. *Swindall.*
Charlotte, Miss *Parsons.*——And Florella, Miss *Smith*

Tickets to be had at the Printing-Office, principal Inns, and of Mr. KNOWLES.

J. TURNER, PRINTER, CIRENCESTER.

Mr. Buckle — I'll thank you to give out
after the 2nd piece as above
"with Good Emphasis & good discretion"

Theatre Bill, 1802.   Courtesy Bingham Library.

Town Map, 1835. Drawn by John Wood.   *Courtesy Bingham Library.*

WHAT TO SEE

- Tontine Building, Cecily Hill.

- Cotswold District Council Offices, Trinity Road (former Poor Law Institution, then Watermoor Hospital).

- Cirencester Lock-up (removed from Gloucester Street to Cotswold District Council Offices).

- Watermoor House – now a private residential home, can be seen from St. Michael's Park, entrance off The Avenue.

- The Bowly Almshouses, Watermoor Road.

- The Querns, now part of the new Cirencester Hospital complex, Tetbury Road.

Victorian Cirencester 1837–1901

The young queen's coronation was celebrated in splendid style in Cirencester. There were firework displays, band concerts, donkey races and triumphal arches in the streets. A 'good substantial dinner' was provided for the poor at which 536 lbs of meat, 564 gallons of beer and 2,200 lbs of pudding were consumed, paid for by public subscription.

Cirencester's population of about 5,500 at the Queen's accession grew to just over 8,000 by the end of the century. Many however continued to live in courts and alleys in the central area of the town. An analysis of the 1851 census returns reveal that over 800 people were living in Cricklade Street. It was only as land was made available to the south-west of the town that there could be any extensive expansion. In 1853 the Chester-Master family offered for sale building plots on the site once occupied by Gregory's nursery. Progress was slow at first but new roads were constructed – Tower Street in 1853, Corin Street (later re–named The Avenue) and New Road (later Victoria Road) in 1859. By 1861 Chester Street and Church Street had been added and in 1870 land on the east site of Victoria Road was also put up for sale. By the last years of the century a variety of housing had been erected in this area, ranging from substantial town villas to semi-detached houses and terraces. The Cirencester Improvement Dwelling Company was founded in 1880, following comments by the local Medical Officer of Health on the bad construction and sanitation of the houses occupied by the poor in some parts of the town. The Company's first venture to provide simple accommodation at a reasonable rental resulted in Victoria Terrace, ten cottages and a shop (now Watermoor Post Office). This was followed by similar housing in Queen Street and School Lane. Earl Bathurst built Apsley Terrace in Watermoor Road and, stimulated by the potential growth of Watermoor with the coming of the railway in 1883, the Improvement Company built the slightly more elaborate Watermoor Villas.

Cottages in Cricklade Street pulled down in 1866.   *Courtesy Bingham Library.*

Tower Street with building in progress on the former Jefferies' Nursery site.
Photo. J. Welsford.

Two other opportunities for major housing development also came in the second half of the century. The sale of the Pitacres estate and other land at Chesterton allowed building in Mount Street and Somerford Road and it is in the latter that there are to be found some of the few examples of the professional man's large town house which exist in Cirencester. In 1890 William Cripps sold off some six acres of the Ashcroft Estate, retaining Ashcroft House and about an acre of land. Ashcroft Road was constructed to link Cricklade Street with Sheep Street and part of the present Ashcroft Gardens and St. Peter's Road (then known as Ashcroft) date from the same period. Here also there was a variety of both brick and stone housing.

As in earlier centuries, Cirencester's economy continued to rely heavily on its position as the market focus for the surrounding countryside for which it provided a wide range of goods and services. Although attempts to revive the wool market were unsuccessful, the corn trade continued to flourish, despite fluctuations caused by wars and foreign and colonial competition. The decision in 1855 to revert to a 'pitched' market accentuated complaints of lack of space – the Market House built by Earl Bathurst in 1819 was no longer adequate and much business was being transacted in the open and in nearby inns such as the White Hart. Fears that such conditions might drive trade away led to the formation of the Corn Hall Company which, with a capital of £3,000, erected in 1862 the Corn Hall and in 1863 the Corn Hall buildings on the site of the old Boothall, leased by Earl Bathurst. The architects of this Italianate building which now graced the Market Place were the respected Medland, Maberly and Medland and the sculptors of the facade were the Forsyth brothers. With the building by Earl Bathurst of the new cattle market in 1867 on the Tetbury Road most livestock transactions were also removed from the Market Place although the annual Christmas poultry market continued to be held there for many years.

The proximity of the Tetbury Road market to the Great Western Railway station was a great advantage for farmers and dealers. Many others benefitted from the improvements in communications during the Victorian era. Although road transport continued to be important particularly in linking nearby towns and villages to Cirencester – in 1876 56 carriers are named in a local Trade Directory – the great age of coach travel was passing. One of the two major coaching inns, the Ram, closed in the

The Corn Hall.   *Photo. A. Welsford.*

Horse trading in the Market Place – a John Beecham lithograph.
Courtesy Bingham Library.

The G.W.R. Station.   *Courtesy Bingham Library.*

1880's and the other, the King's Head, retained its commercial viability by developing facilities for the increasing number of visitors during the hunting season and by providing transport to and from the station for its guests. The G.W.R. branch line to Kemble linking Cirencester to London and the south-west was opened in 1841, the journey to London taking six hours. Cheaper travel was brought within the means of more people who could take advantage of day excursions such as that to visit the Great Exhibition in 1851, for a first class return fare of 17 shillings or 13 shillings for a second class ticket. School children from local schools were also taken by train to the capital. In 1883 opportunities for rail travel were increased when the Midland and South Western Joint Railway reached the town. The opening of its station at Watermoor in the following year linked Cirencester with the South Coast and the Midlands. Traffic on the Thames and Severn Canal, not surprisingly, declined – particularly after the canal was bought out by the G.W.R. in 1882 – and although coal merchants continued to operate from the old canal wharf, many of their supplies came by road or rail. In 1887 it was reported that during the year only 17 vessels had used the canal, making a total of 14 trips with cargoes of Bristol road stone, sawdust, bricks and gravel.

The advent of the railways and the railway carriage works at Watermoor brought employment to the town replacing some of the jobs lost through the decline of the coaching traffic. Fewer people were employed in agriculture although the agricultural interest remained strong and was stimulated by the foundation of the Agricultural College in 1845. This opened in temporary accommodation in Thomas Street and was then transferred to the impressive building on the Tetbury Road. Numbers involved in textile manufacture also declined. By 1842 both Cripps' mill at Stratton and the Silks' carpet factory in Gloucester Street had closed, with the loss of about 170 jobs. By 1880 only four firms were employed in the once extensive wool stapling business. In the 1851 census returns only 48 people were connected with textile and allied crafts such as rope-making.

There was, of course, some manufacturing industry – particularly of tools and agricultural implements and machinery. The edge-tool manufacture for which the town was said once to have had a national reputation continued until the 1870's. The foundry established by Henry Alexander in 1849 in Cricklade Street was the basis of a successful business which in 1871 was employing 35 men. Wound up in 1883, the firm was taken over by a former manager, John Delve, transferred to Watermoor, and later continued as Juke's foundry. There are references to other foundries – one in Dyer Street and another, the Suffolk Iron Works, in Lewis Lane. In the latter part of the century the manufacture of agricultural implements was carried on by the Webbs' works. Carriage building was undertaken by firms such as those of Cock and of Millington and the increasing popularity of cycling led to the existence of a number of cycle manufacturers. Other work could be found at the major breweries of Cripps and Bowly (taken over by Cripps in 1882), at the flour and flock mills, the Cole and Lewis bacon factory or the Gas Works. Many of the largest employers of labour, however, were builders, reflecting the expansion of the town. In 1861, for example, Bridges, the builders, were employing 90 men. A number of people were engaged in large retail establishments, like those of drapers such as Boultons or Hydes. Some came from nearby villages or even further away and lived on the premises, usually in the attics. A high proportion of the labour force was in domestic service – with wages at a low level even a modest

People in DOMESTIC SERVICE in CIRENCESTER in 1881 From the Census

WOMEN

General Servant	242
Laundress	70
Housemaid	56
Cook	46
Housekeeper	28
Nurse	21
Charwoman	17
Kitchen maid	14
Nursemaid/Undernurse	13
Parlourmaid	10
Governess	8
Lady's maid	8
Barmaid	4
Chambermaid	2
Schoolroom maid	2
Waitress	2
Undercook	1
Stillroom maid	1
Dairy maid	1
Scullery maid	1
Mother's help	1

MEN

Groom	68
Gardener	43
Coachman	19
Butler	9
Footman	9
Ostler	7
Page – 6 at R.A.C	7
General Servant	5
Waiter	3
Valet	2
Stableman	2
Underboots	2
Boots	1
Underwaiter	1
Gardener's boy	1
General Servant (boy)	1
Porter	1

TOTAL POPULATION, 7737 of which 649 (8.4%) in Domestic Service

Domestic Servants in Cirencester 1881.   *Chart. A. & J. Welsford.*

household could afford the assistance of a girl in her teens while the more prosperous classes would have maintained a staff of at least three or more.

Working hours were long and employment not always secure. Writing of his father who had a plumbing and decorating business in Castle Street, the historian Kennet J. Beecham remarks that he was very kind in keeping on his regular men during the winter months, implying that this was not a regular practice. Trade Unions were illegal until the 1870's but there is occasional evidence of concerted action as in 1865 when the carpenters and joiners employed by Mr. Bridges on the parish church restoration struck for a weekly increase of 4 shillings on the £1 they were earning for a 59 hour week. They claimed that they were not earning sufficient to cope with the high price of meat and house rent as they were working on piece rates on very hard wood. In times of hardship there was of course no national scheme of unemployment or sickness pay. Some workers joined Friendly Societies or Benefit Societies such as the Oddfellows or the Ancient Order of Foresters. In return for a weekly subscription they could obtain some assistance when required. Since the Poor Law Amendment Act of 1834 there was little 'outdoor' relief for those unable to fend for themselves. In extreme cases a family would be compelled to enter the Union Workhouse at Watermoor. Here men, women and children were housed separately, the able-bodied adults were put to gainful occupation and the children educated to 'fulfil their duty in the state of life in which they may be placed'. Local philanthropists sought to alleviate hardship by setting up a Soup Kitchen (in 1865) and Medical, Coal and Clothing Clubs. Charities set up by earlier generations continued to assist some of the poor by providing almshouses, clothing and apprenticeship fees.

Another problem of much concern to nineteenth century reformers was that of excessive consumption of alcohol particularly among the working classes. Although some of Cirencester's public houses had been closed at the beginning of the century, the town had many more than today and Temperance Reformers, often Non-Conformists, such as Christopher Bowly and Henry Alexander sought to curtail their influence. In 1846, Christopher Bowly erected the Temperance Hall in Thomas Street, ironically on the site of a former brewery, while a little later Henry Alexander established a tee-total Working Men's Club in premises in Cricklade Street. Commercial enterprises such as the Globe

The Temperance Hall, Thomas Street.   *Photo. A. Welsford.*

Temperance Hotel in Castle Street, the Temperance Coffee House and the Cotswold Coffee Tavern were other attempts to beat the demon, drink.

Men such as Bowly and Alexander were typical of the wealthy entrepreneurial middle class, combining an astute business sense with a concern for the town and its inhabitants. Names

135

Jefferies' Corner before widening in 1897.   *Courtesy Bingham Library.*

from families such as the Cripps, the Bowlys and the Brewins were usually to be found on subscription lists, associated with enterprises like the Permanent Library or turning their own enthusiasms to the general advantage as in the example of Wilfrid Cripps, a keen amateur archaeologist, whose private museum of Roman antiquities was later donated to the Corinium Museum. The Bathurst family continued to be natural leaders in the community, although their influence as Lords of the Manor declined with nineteenth century government legislation. Ves-

STATEMENT OF RECEIPTS AND EXPENDITURE,

From January 1st, 1850, to January 1st, 1851.

	£.	s.	d.		£.	s	d.
Paid George Giles for repairing, watering, and cleansing the Streets....	110	6	5	By Amount received on account of three rates at 8d. in the pound....	825	19	5
......for stone (Bristol)..	62	19	6	.........Churchwardens' Interest on £1000 applied towards re-building the Town Hall, one year to Lady-day, 1850.	40	0	0
......labour, breaking ditto	14	2	11	........Rent of stalls and stallage................	45	5	0
......for pitching, paving, and guttering	73	13	1	.........On account of side drains....................	19	10	6
......Cleansing brooks..	10	5	4	Balance due to Treasurer 1st January. 1851..................	507	18	10
......Working fire engines, one year's pay	7	0	0	......ditto Surveyors' ditto	50	0	0
......Repairing ditto..	3	7	6				
......Carpenters' and Smiths' Bills, ...	12	11	1				
......Repairs of lamps and painting	8	14	2				
......Making common sewer in Gloucester and Coxwell Streets.	149	0	9				
......Messrs Bravender and Trinder for Plan and Surveying	20	0	0				
......Incidental payments.	22	3	6				
......Churchwardens, one year's reserved rent of Mr. Acott's late house.	0	10	0				
......Powell's Charity, Mr. Habgood's ditto	5	19	0				
......Rent of premises for stone yard......................	1	17	6				
......Messrs. Bowly, Coles, and others, on account of Annuity on £2000.	109	4	0				
......Printing and Stationery	16	3	0				
......Salary and other payments to Clerk	26	15	0				
......Ditto, Collector of Rates	17	10	0				
......Ditto, Inspector of Nuisances.......................	10	0	0				
......Mr. Anderson, Bailiwick Fees, (Seven Quarters)........	45	17	4				
......Land Tax. &c..	8	16	8				
......Gas Company, one year's contract, and two extra Lamps in Lewis Lane	229	0	0				
......Ditto, extra lighting ....….........	7	15	8				
......Banker's Commission, Interest, &c.	23	13	8				
......Balance due to Surveyors. 1st January, 1850.................	14	9	2				
...... ,, ,, Treasurer, ditto	466	14	10				
£	1488	13	9	£	1488	13	9

TOWN HALL, CIRENCESTER, JANUARY 29, 1851.

Signed on behalf of the Commissioners present, at a Meeting held this Day.

DANIEL SEALY, CHAIRMAN.

The Town Improvement Commissioners' Accounts 1851.

Courtesy Bingham Library.

tiges of the old manorial government remained. The High Steward and High Bailiff of the Manor were the returning officers at parliamentary elections and the High Steward often presided at public meetings. Each town ward continued to elect annually two wardsmen and the Court Leet met at least until 1914, appointing honorary officers such as carnals, ale-tasters and water-bailiffs. The Bathurst involvement ranged from the offering of prizes at local agricultural shows to the provision of the town's museum in 1856 and the Cottage Hospital in 1875. Richard Jefferies, the naturalist, who was a reporter on the Wilts. and Gloucestershire Standard, in his description of Fleeceborough (which is Cirencester thinly disguised) in 'Hodge and his Masters' refers to 'the substantial assistance to any and every movement set on foot by the respectable men', given by 'he' (i.e. the Earl).

Cirencester was not incorporated under the Municipal Cor-

porations' Act of 1835 and the Town Commissioners continued
to be responsible for the everyday running of affairs until 1876.
An Inspector of Nuisances was appointed at an annual salary of
£10 and later replaced by a Sanitary Officer. Prosecutions were
brought for badly constructed privies, night soil carts without
proper flushboards and for pigs on domestic premises. Although
the town was unaffected by the cholera epidemics of the 1840's
and 1850's, an outbreak of scarlet fever in 1870 resulted in 55
deaths and was openly attributed to defective housing, sanitation and water supply. All water came from wells and springs
and, although borings in the Barton area showed that piped
water could be taken from here, the suggestion was not followed
up. This was probably because of lack of finacial resources – the
Commissioners had already in 1865, been forced to advertise for
people willing to lend them a total of £1,000 to improve the
paving in the town. Nor was much done to deal with the
intermittent flooding which occurred in some parts. This was
particularly bad in 1870 when residents in Gloucester Street
complained of water up to a foot deep in their cellars. It was said
that this was caused by the ancient custom of irrigating the
meadows behind and it was recommended that the practice
should cease. Heavy rainfall could also seriously affect the water
levels in the Churn and subsidiary streams. On occasions there
could be a difference of twelve feet between the water level at
Gloucester Street Bridge and the Abbey lake, the nearest open
water.

Drainage was one of the problems taken up by the Local
Government Board which replaced the Town Commissioners in
1876. This new body had an extended jurisdiction over the
whole parish of Cirencester except the tithing of Wiggold and
certain parts of Barton and Oakley. For the first time in its history
Cirencester had an election for its local representatives. All male
ratepayers were eligible to vote and the fifteen seats were keenly
contested as the surviving election literature illustrates. In the
eighteen years of its existence the Board accomplished much.
Between 1878–80 Thomas Bravender, its surveyor, put a drainage scheme into operation and a sewage farm was opened on 53
acres at Tudmoor. However, the initiative in the provision of a
water supply had been lost. In 1882 the Cirencester Water Works
Company was founded on the site of Bowly's Brewery in Lewis
Lane with a service reservoir in Bathurst Park. The Board opened
an Infectious Diseases Hospital on the south side of the town,

CIRENCESTER RACES.

LOCAL BOARD STAKES

LATEST BETTING.

Even	on	Posh (bar Cramp)
2 to 1	against	Theodolite
3	„	Jovial Joe
4	„	The Barton Pet
8	„	XXX
10	„	Putty
10	„	The People's Bill
10	„	The Ladies' Doctor
15	„	The Shepherd
15	„	The Blooming Bridegroom
20	„	The Miller
20	„	The Musical Quaker
20	„	The Thunderbolt
25	„	Calico Jack
25	„	The Bumptious Builder
25	„	Chesterton Ch'rlie
30	„	Lump Coal
30	„	The Farmer
40	„	The Squeaking Chemist
50	„	The Union Doctor
60	„	Thin Cheese
60	„	The Old 'Oss
70	„	The Iron Duke
75	„	Holy Billy
100	„	Rev. Small Coal
100	„	(Elect)roplate
100	„	Commodore Nutt
100	„	Double-faced John
200	„	The Tippling Templar
500	„	The Meddling Mercer
1000	„	Drysoil Robert
1000	„	Rags and Bones
1000	„	Joey Treacle
1000	„	Lord Nelson
1000	„	Toady Giglamps

Local Government Elections 1876 – a racing list!   *Courtesy Bingham Library.*

near the canal, took over many of the streets in the Watermoor and former Nursery area and purchased a steam roller for £400. Cricklade Street was widened at the famous 'dog-leg bend'.

In 1894 the Local Government Board was itself replaced by the Cirencester Urban District Council which managed the town's affairs until 1974. Once again the elections were keen contests. The franchise was now extended to all male householders and out of a possible electorate of 1,400–1,500, 1,127 recorded votes. The Urban District Council purchased the Waterworks in 1898 for £16,000 and superintended the widening of Castle Street in 1897 when the present buildings from the former Jefferies' corner in the Market Place to the Post Office were erected. From 1897 until 1932 the Council met here in the Municipal Offices and no longer in the Town Hall.

Changes also occurred in Cirencester's parliamentary representation. After 1867 only one member was sent and the parish of Stratton was henceforth included in the electorate. In 1885 the town lost separate representation and became one of the five Gloucestershire county divisions. In that year a Liberal candidate, Arthur Winterbotham, was returned. Until then, with one or two exceptions, as an anonymous writer of an 1848 pamphlet commented, the town 'was remarkable for the Tory tendency of her views'. Members of the Bathurst and Chester-Master family were often elected and the middle class commercial and professional classes were also in evidence. Joseph Cripps who had been a member for the borough continuously since 1818 was succeeded by his son, William, in 1842. When William died in 1848 his place was taken by the influential local solicitor, Joseph Mullings. There was no secret ballot until 1872 and Mullings' campaign expenses included £5 towards the setting up of the hustings in the Market Place.

The general expansion of educational opportunities in the nineteenth century affected Cirencester also. The Blue and Yellow Schools were amalgamated as Powell's Schools in 1876 and a new school was built next to the original school house which was converted into staff accommodation. The Infant Schoolroom, completed in 1863, continued in use. By 1853 both Watermoor National School and the British Schools in Sheep Street were open and there was another Infant School in Thomas Street. There were also a number of private establishments, such as that of Richard Webb in Coxwell Street, which catered for the more well-to-do. The educational legislation of the 1870's permitted the setting up of Local School Boards, empowered to levy a rate to provide free undenominational elementary education. Education was also compulsory from 1880. The Cirencester Board Schools – for Boys, Girls and Mixed Infants – were opened in 1879 in purpose–built accommodation in Lewis Lane. At the

CIRENCESTER LOCAL BOARD.

Wilts and Gloucestershire Standard Office,
Saturday, October 28, 1876.

The Returning Officer, JOHN MULLINGS, Esq.,
declares the following to be the

STATE OF THE POLL:—

BRAVENDER, JOHN	1131
SEWELL, JOSEPH	1119
ANDERSON, ROBERT A.	1099
CRIPPS, FREDERICK	931
CLARK, WILLIAM	927
BEECHAM, JOHN	853
TRINDER, EDWARD	753
LAWRENCE, CHARLES WM.	750
ZACHARY, HENRY	745
CRIPPS, EDWARD	743
BURGESS, JOHN	727
SMITH, CHARLES S.	687
WARNER, THOMAS	639
ALEXANDER, HENRY	553
BOWLY, CHRISTOPHER	549
HARMER, GEORGE HENRY	463
COLE, RICHARD	425
JAMES, WILLIAM HENRY	415
SMITH, JOSEPH	407
MILLER, JOHN	355
ALLEN, ROBERT	350
HYDE, JOHN	321
HODGES, WILLIAM	308
FARRELL, GEORGE	179
COLE, WILLIAM	178
FREEMAN, ROBERT C.	172
BOWLY, JAMES EDWARD	157
NEWCOMBE, WILLIAM	130
HISCOCK, JOHN	117
BARNARD, THOMAS	116
AUSTIN, HENRY	99
GEGG, JOSEPH	94
PRICE, THOMAS	79

The first fifteen gentlemen will form the
Local Board.

Elections 1876 – Successful candidates.   *Courtesy Bingham Library.*

same time the British Schools and the Infant School in Thomas Street closed.

The fortunes of Cirencester's Grammar School fluctuated during this period. A government report of 1869 commented on the state of disrepair and the small number of pupils – 25 day and 7 boarders, 3 of whom had not returned three weeks after the beginning of term! The decision was taken to found an Upper School for Boys incorporating money from the Powell's Trust with Grammar School resources. The Upper School opened in 1881 in new buildings in Victoria Road under the leadership of the Rev. G.R. Faulkener. Although the beginning was not particularly propitious – there were 16 boys in three classrooms and a large schoolroom with a lavatory that at first had no water supply – within a few years the school had re-established its reputation. Additional rooms were provided and the school later reverted to its former title of 'Grammar'.

Another new educational institution was the School of Art which began in 1860 in Dyer Street and transferred in 1863 to the Corn Hall. In origin it owed much to contemporary emphasis on the importance of industrial design stimulated by the Great Exhibition of 1851 and was affiliated to the Science and Art Department at South Kensington from which it received an annual grant. The first Art Master, James Miller, was also Professor of Drawing at the Agricultural College and under his energetic direction the School flourished. Instruction was also given to local school children and railway workers at Swindon. Several pupils, such as members of the Gibbons' family and Samuel Llewellyn, later President of the Royal Academy, achieved national recognition. However, in the 1880's numbers declined and the school closed in 1901.

Self help and self improvement were popular Victorian concepts and organisations like the Mechanics' Institutes aimed at helping their members by lectures and library facilities. The Cirencester branch was founded in 1844 with a membership of tradesmen and a few professional men. One of those most active in its cause was John Beecham who often gave lectures and whose house at 15 Park Street was for some time the home of its 500 volume library. There was another subscription library in Cirencester, founded in 1835 in Dyer Street as the Permanent Library and Subscription Rooms. In its early years this achieved a modest success but then public support dwindled and by 1859 it was being run by a local bookseller, Baily. Interest revived

Notice of Lecture given by John Beecham. *Courtesy Bingham Library.*

FOR ONE NIGHT ONLY.

CORN HALL, CIRENCESTER.

THE MEMBERS OF THE

CIRENCESTER CRICKET CLUB

ASSISTED BY

Mr. T. B. SHENTON, of Cheltenham,

WILL GIVE AN

AMATEUR DRAMATIC ENTERTAINMENT

In the above Hall,

On Wednesday, December 9, 1868,

IN AID OF THE FUNDS OF THE CLUB,

A heavy Debt having been incurred by providing Accommodation for Spectators at Cricket Matches.

The Performances will commence with the COMIC DRAMA of

THE

SPECTRE BRIDEGROOM,

Or, A GHOST IN SPITE OF HIMSELF.

Mr. Nicodemus	Mr. FRANK HOARE.
Squire Aldwinkle	Mr. T. B. SHENTON.
Captain Vauntington	Mr. A. E. BARTLETT.
Dickory	Mr. W. PARRY.
Paul	Mr. C. HAWKINS.
Thomas	Mr. C. BOULTON.

To be followed by a

MISCELLANEOUS CONCERT.

SONG	" Come into the Garden Maud "	Mr. G. GREENWOOD.
COMIC SONG	"The Blighted Barber, or, Fe, Fi, Fo, Fum "	Mr. F. CLAPPEN.
SONG	"Stonewall Jackson "	Mr. W. J. GREENWOOD.
SONG	"The Valiant Knight "	Mr. T. SKINNER.
COMIC SONG	"Good-bye John "	Mr. JOE MATTHEWS.
SONG	'I'm Afloat "	Mr. C. GREEN.

To conclude with the MUSICAL FARCE of

THE REVIEW,

Or, THE WAGS OF WINDSOR.

Mr. Deputy Bull *(a retired Grocer)*	Mr. C. HAWKINS.
Captain Beaugard	Mr. T. SQUIRES.
Caleb Quotem *(with Songs)*	Mr. G. GREENWOOD.
Looney Mactwolter *(an Irishman)*	Mr. FRANK HOARE.
John Lump *(a Countryman)*	Mr. W. PARRY.
Dubbs *(servant to Quotem)*	Mr. C. BOULTON.
Page *(to Mr. Bull)*	Mr. W. GOSTLING.

Stage Manager	Mr. T. B. SHENTON.
Leader of the Band	Mr. E. YATES.

Prices of Admission—Reserved Seats, 2s.; Unreserved Seats, 1s.

The Box Office will be open at BAILY'S LIBRARY on Monday, December 7th, at 11 o'clock, where a Plan of the Room may be seen and Places Secured.

The Entrance to Reserved Seats will be at the Front Door, and to Unreserved Seats at the Side Door of the Hall.

Doors open at 7.30, to commence at 8 o'clock. *Carriages (at Front Door), may be ordered for a Quarter-past Ten.*

BAILY, PRINTER, CIRENCESTER.

Theatre Bill – Corn Hall.   *Courtesy Bingham Library.*

with the opening of the Corn Hall buildings. The shareholders joined their stock with that of the Mechanics' Institute and the Library was transferred to the Corn Hall. A range of facilities was offered for annual subscriptions from 21 shillings to 5 shillings. Well patronized at first, by 1884 public interest had again diminished and the Reading Room was given up. In the following year even after a sale of books there remained only £12 in the funds. Once again Messrs. Baily took over the management.

Perhaps the stock of the library was not sufficiently attractive, especially to those newly literate. However, there were many other available leisure activities. The Corn Hall was the venue for both amateur and professional theatrical companies. The Assembly Rooms at the King's Head also offered professional entertainers – illusionists, ventriloquists and dancers as well as the more conventional balls and concerts. Visiting circuses and zoos were popular and on one occasion traffic in the Market Place was completely disrupted by a number of camels advertising a travelling menagerie. There were fireworks and band concerts in the Market Place, and royal occasions such as the marriage of the Prince of Wales in 1863 provided opportunities for public festivities. The Mop or Hiring Fair was an annual attraction. At this, until 1862, agricultural labourers, ploughmen, carters and shepherds and young women hoping to get a good place in domestic service stood in the Market Place, but in that year this activity was transferred to the Corn Hall. The stalls, roundabouts and side shows, however, remained in the Market Place until the 1960's. Steam roundabouts were at first forbidden because of the noise. The fun usually began at midnight on the Sunday prior to the Monday mop. When the church clock struck twelve, horses were set in motion from outside the town in a rush to obtain the best pitch and hold it against all comers. Later the showmen were allowed to settle places before midnight and in 1928 it was agreed to book places in advance.

Cirencester could also provide a range of sporting activities – the Cricket Club, founded in 1842, played in Cirencester Park and on occasion was strong enough to beat an all England XI. Tennis, archery and football were also popular and many visitors, including the Prince of Wales in 1877, came to the town for the hunting season. The Swimming Baths Company formed in 1870, provided the open air swimming pool beside the Gunstool Brook which is still in use today. Cirencester Park was open to the public and there was skating on its lake when weather

Celebrations for the wedding of Edward VII as Prince of Wales in 1863.
Courtesy Bingham Library.

permitted. Societies like the Microscopical Society and the Cotteswold Naturalist Club catered for the more academically minded and in 1862 a group of well-meaning gentlemen inaugurated the Penny Readings in the Corn Hall. These continued on a regular basis for almost ten years.

For many children, apart from the excitement of the mop, the highlights of the year would have been the Sunday School Christmas party and summer outing – perhaps a picnic tea in the Park or on Minchinhampton Common, travelling by horse-drawn wagonette. Church and Chapel were still significant in the lives of many and religious matters could arouse heated controversy. The Rev. William Powell, vicar of the parish church, found that his attempts to introduce High Church innovations were not popular with all. He referred in his letters to a mob which followed him in the street 'hooting, yelling and jeering' and he eventually dismissed the church organist for persistently refusing to play the tunes Powell requested. It was William Powell who masterminded the restoration work in the parish church. The eighteenth century high pews and galleries were removed and the organ taken from the top of the chancel screen. In 1865 the major scheme was begun under the direction of Sir George Gilbert Scott. The staircase leading from the Trinity Chapel was removed and the Chapel became an annexe to the nave. All the floors were taken up and the nave aisle repaired with red tiles instead of stone. The old porch house was demolished and the Abbey wall set back, thus opening up the north side of the church.

The spiritual needs of the growing district of Watermoor were met by the building of Holy Trinity Church. Consecrated in 1851 this was also the work of Sir George Gilbert Scott. There was much building activity by the Nonconformists. The Baptist Chapel in Coxwell Street was rebuilt in 1856–7. Another Separatist Baptist Chapel opened in 1854 in Park Street under the ministry of the Rev. Henry Tanner. The Independent or Congregational Chapel was founded in Sheep Street in 1839. The minister here was the Rev. Joseph Stratford, author of 'Great and Good Men of Gloucestershire'. A schoolroom was added to the Wesleyan Methodist Chapel in Gloucester Street and a Primitive Methodist Chapel was built in Lewis Lane in 1851. Both the Methodist Chapel in Ashcroft Road and St. Peter's Roman Catholic Church date from 1896 and the opening up of the Ashcroft estate. Before this the Roman Catholic community

Cirencester from the Tetbury Road, showing the nineteenth century police
station and magistrates' court.   *Courtesy Bingham Library.*

Watermoor Church.   *Courtesy Bingham Library.*

Ashcroft Methodist Church, founded 1896.   *Photo. A. Welsford.*

worshipped at a chapel in the London Road, now barely reveal-
ing its former function. The Salvation Army held its first open-
air meeting in the town in 1881 and although initially had some
violent opponents, was accepted within a few years.

The street violence which erupted during early Salvation
Army meetings was not altogether unusual in Cirencester. Cirencester's police force which was first established in 1839 in a
house in Gloucester Street and in 1859 transferred to new
premises in Castle Street, seems to have been accustomed to
dealing with many street disturbances. Cases of drunkeness were
not uncommon nor were fights when the protagonists were often
encouraged by a large crowd. In 1867 the North Wilts. Herald
reported a large number of prosecutions for offences on 5th
November. Many fireworks had been let off illegally and some
200 'roughs of the town' had thrown stones at the police. In the
words of Police Sergeant Eyles 'it was as bad as an election day'.
A few years earlier militiamen had clashed with police in the
Market Place and what might have been a very ugly incident was
only defused by the police superintendent and militia officers.
This provoked letters in the Wilts. and Gloucestershire Standard
bewailing the 'pernicious effect' of the militiamen on the 'moral
condition of the people' and saying that it was quite unsafe for

any respectable female to walk out of an evening.

The militiamen in question were part of the Royal North Gloucester Militia, first raised in 1757. In 1881 this became the 4th Battalion of the Gloucestershire regiment. From 1854–6 the militiamen were quartered in the town, billeted on the town-speople. Thereafter from 1859 they assembled in the town each year for training and were housed in the Barracks on Cecily Hill, erected in 1856. Cirencester also had a volunteer Rifle Corps. but this was disbanded just before the Boer War. The 4th Battalion of the Gloucestershires saw active service in that war, entraining from the G.W.R. station in the town. By the time the war was over in 1902, Queen Victoria's long reign was also over and England and Cirencester had entered the twentieth century.

WHAT TO SEE

• Market Place – Corn Hall and King's Head (the latter has a Victorian facade although the hotel dates back to the sixteenth century).

• Temperance Hall, now Salvation Army Temple, Thomas Street.

• The Barracks, Cecily Hill.

• The Baptist Chapel, Coxwell Street.

• The former Police Station and Magistrates' Court, Castle Street/Park Lane.

• The Royal Agricultural College, Tetbury Road.

• Holy Trinity Church, Watermoor.

• Former Grammar School Building, Victoria Road.

Cirencester in the Twentieth Century

Few people living in Cirencester when Edward VII came to the throne in 1901 would have remembered a time when Queen Victoria was not the reigning monarch. Since her accession sixty-four years before momentous changes had taken place in the social and political structure of a Britain which had become the workshop of the world and a great imperial power. Although Cirencester had remained basically a market town and, as Beecham in 1910 said 'a noted agricultural centre, encouraged by the Royal Agricultural College of world-wide fame', fewer people than formerly were engaged in agricultural employment. 'In years gone by men went from the town to the villages to work, now this is reversed'.

This trend was reflected nationally in the agricultural depression of the later years of the nineteenth century which was caused by a series of bad harvests, harsh foreign competition from the opening up of the North American Prairies and faster and cheaper shipping. Whereas in 1851 agriculture accounted for 20.3% of the national income, by 1901 its share had fallen to 6.4% and much food and raw materials such as wool were being imported. Politicians were not unaware of the problem – in his election address in 1895 the Hon. Ben Bathurst, the Unionist candidate had pledged all necessary and moderate reform to alleviate agricultural distress and the trade depression. Successful like his party at this election, Ben Bathurst and the Unionists succumbed in 1906 to the Liberal challenge of Free Trade against their campaign for a return to a policy of Protection. William Essex replaced Bathurst as the member for Cirencester and Tewkesbury.

Included in the new Liberal government's programme were measures for the greater well-being of children such as the provision of school medical examinations and medical services. The log book of the Girls' Council School in Lewis Lane records in September 1908 that, at the very first examination, seventy-

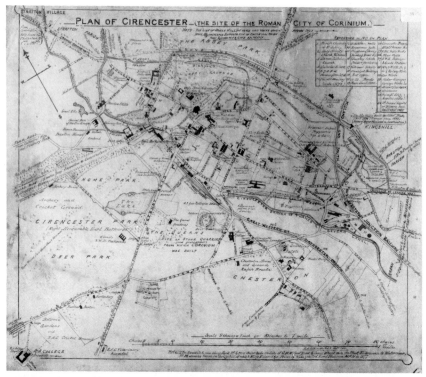

Kennet Beecham's Plan of Cirencester, 1911.   *Courtesy Bingham Library.*

two children were seen, eighteen of whom were leaving and the rest were described as 'exceptional cases'. Voluntary bodies, however, were still active, as the minutes of the Cirencester Child Care Committee founded in 1911 illustrate. Using money from local subscriptions, milk was supplied to schools at a low rate and free to the very poor. Saucepans for heating milk and mugs were also provided and occasionally Virol and Scotts' Emulsion for particularly delicate children. Medical treatment, eye tests and spectacles were paid for if necessary. The Committee continued its work until 1936 when Gloucestershire Education Committee assumed responsibility for such services.

Even for poorer children there were welcome diversions. Annual holidays were given for Nutting in Cirencester Park, for Sunday School treats, for Mop and when the circus came to town. On 24th May, Queen Victoria's birthday, which was

152

observed as Empire Day, there was usually a special celebration. In 1906 the girls at the Council School marched to the Market Place sang the National Anthem and the 'Flag of Britain' and then had a half holiday. In later years they hoisted their own flag, presented by the Hon. Ben Bathurst, at their own school and were given buns and oranges. In June 1911, children had an extra week's holiday in honour of the coronation of George V and a fortnight later yet another half holiday to take part in the Coronation sports which had been postponed because of bad weather.

For the adult poor and unemployed there was no financial assistance other than that provided by their families, local charities or Friendly Societies, until the government in 1908 introduced Old Age Pensions, giving five shillings a week to people over seventy with incomes of less than £31-10s per annum, and the first National Insurance Act in 1911. The Cirencester Board of Guardians, established under the Poor Law Amendment Act of 1834, was still responsible for the adminis-tration of local relief from the rates and the Union Workhouse. Vagrancy appears to have been a problem. In 1903, concerned at the large number of vagrants, the Cirencester Board considered a scheme to send tramps to labour colonies for three years to be taught to work. Earlier in the same year two tramps had been committed for twenty-one days hard labour for refusing to break stones at the Workhouse. Possibly because of the government reforms the number of paupers receiving relief declined some-what in the early years of the century. In 1901 a total of 209 had been assisted – 72 in the Workhouse and 137 outside – by weekly financial payments. In 1912 numbers had fallen to 139 – of these 62 were inmates and 77 had been given 'outdoor' relief.

The tradition of private philanthropy was continued by Daniel Bingham, who in 1905 founded and endowed the public library in the building now known as Bingham House, the present offices of Cirencester Town Council. Born in Black Jack Street in 1830 the son of a cabinet maker, Daniel Bingham became a clerk at Cirencester G.W.R. Station and then, at the age of twenty-five, moved to Paddington with his immediate superior, James Staat Forbes. When the latter went to Holland to re-organise the Dutch-Rhenish railways, Bingham accompanied him and within a few years when Forbes retired, took over the operation. In Holland Daniel Bingham amassed a considerable fortune by judicious investment and although he made his permanent home in Utrecht, he did not forget his native town. Having subscribed for a number of years to the ailing Public Library in the Corn Hall, he offered to establish a totally new institution at a personal cost of some £50,000. Hailed by contemporaries as 'Cirencester's Carnegie', in some ways Bingham was even more enlightened since he not only erected the building but invested money to provide for its running costs and the services of a professional librarian. The new Library, designed by the well known local architect V.A. Lawson, contained in addition to reference and lending facilities, a Reading Room, a Smoking and Games Room, a Lecture Room and a Gymnasium. A wide range of newspapers and periodicals and free stationery was supplied for the Reading Room, and the Games Room, where draughts and chess were played, was opened on Sunday afternoons and evenings. Classes in Physical Education and Needlework were organised at Daniel Bingham's expense and a series of free lectures was so popular – nearly 500 people attended the first meeting – that the Lecture Room proved too small and the Corn Hall was hired. The Library itself was also popular with 1,299 people registering as borrowers in its first year. The success of the lectures inspired Daniel Bingham to build and endow the Bingham Hall in 1908. This, with its adjoining Rifle Range, was given to the town under the management of a group of Trustees. In addition to providing a venue for lectures, concerts and dramatic performances, in its early years it also housed exhibitions organised by local societies.

The early twentieth century brought increased educational opportunities for women. The Cirencester Girls' High School was founded in 1901 in premises in The Avenue. In 1904 it moved to the Grammar School site in Victoria Road. The Grammar School buildings here had already been extended in 1900 and now an extra wing was added. The girls' department, however, remained quite separate for many years. Former pupils remember the high fence which divided the boys' and girls' playgrounds and boys and girls were required to use different routes to and from school. Women also began to play a more active role in politics. In Cirencester there were Women's Unionist and Women's Liberal Associations and the question of women's suffrage aroused interest. Both supporters and opponents of the extension of the right to vote were represented in branches of the law-abiding National Union of Women's Suffrage Societies and the National League for Opposing Women's Suffrage.

154

Bingham Villas, King Street. Built by Daniel Bingham as part of the endowment for the Bingham Hall.   *Photo. A. Welsford.*

Other twentieth century developments had an impact on the town. The delights of the early cinema could be experienced at the Picture House in the Market Place approached by a side passage next to the Corn Hall, and the very beginnings of later traffic problems are noticeable when Gloucestershire County Council asked the Urban District Council for its views on a speed restriction of 10 m.p.h. There was general agreement to this although some members thought it was too fast! Council discussions on the provision of dwelling houses in 1902 led to the purchase of a 2½ acre site between Gas House Lane and Siddington Road. By 1912 twenty-four houses had been completed.

Any further such developments were interrupted by the 1914–18 war. Items on the Council's agenda in August 1914 included the siting of guns to protect the reservoir and the placing of an air-raid hooter on Cripps' Brewery. Fortunately there was little enemy air activity in the district since the hooter appears to have not been very effective. Towards the end of the war when there was a threat of daytime raids, it was suggested that men on bicycles carrying placards should notify the population as half an hour would elapse between the initial warning and the enemy arrival. The Mop was cancelled for the duration of the war and

Cirencester Grammar School.

Advertisement for the Girls' Grammar School.   *Courtesy Bingham Library.*

four farmers were co-opted onto a special council sub-committee to speed up food production.

Many members of the armed forces including men from the South Wales Borderers, 10th Gordon Highlanders and 7th Cameroons were stationed in the town, billeted in private homes or in halls such as the Corn Hall and Apsley Hall in Sheep Street. A battalion of Gloucestershire Yeomanry was encamped in Cirencester Park. The Bingham Hall was used as a Red Cross Hospital. Opened in 1914, in its first year it admitted 404 patients who were received at Watermoor Station from the disembarcation ports and Tidworth Military Hospital. Concerts and other entertainments were arranged for the troops and the Librarian, Sidney Harrison, obtained their local home newspapers and organised French classes. Other concerts were held in aid of Belgian refugees whose plight was very much taken to heart by the town. In 1916 the pupils at the Girls' Council School asked that money normally expended on their annual prizes should be given to help Belgian children.

National Reserve Church Parade, 1912.   *Courtesy Bingham Library.*

The ending of the war in November 1918 was received in the words of the Wilts. and Gloucestershire Standard with 'heartfelt joy and gladness'. The bells rang out, steam whistles and hooters heralded the happy event and as darkness fell, rockets and maroons illuminated the sky. The mood of celebration was tempered by the thoughts of those who would not return – the 209 whose names are recorded on the war memorial by the parish church. Another tangible reminder was the Memorial Hospital in Sheep Street, built on the site of the former Congregational Church. Cirencester 'adopted' two French villages, Passel and Ville, south of Amiens, which had been devastated in the fighting. Organised by Countess Bathurst, money was raised to purchase household goods, a clock for Ville, a bell for Passel and fruit trees to re-stock gardens.

Over the next few years Cirencester acquired additional amenities. Twenty-four more council houses were soon completed in Chesterton Lane, playing fields were opened at City Bank and the Bowls Club found its home in Ashcroft. In 1931 the open-air Swimming Baths, the property of the Urban District Council since 1896, were refurbished. The new Baunton pumping station was inaugurated in 1936 although some houses in the town still relied on wells for water. Electricity had been supplied in

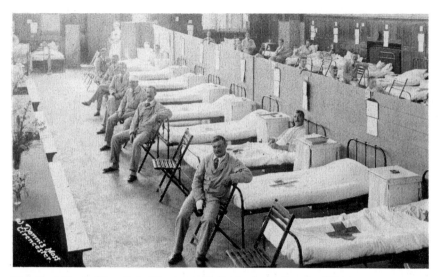

The Red Cross Hospital, Bingham Hall, during 1914–18 War.
Courtesy Corinium Museum.

Cirencester since 1912 but it was only after the 1914–18 war that
it was used for public street lighting. At Christmas 1927, the
inmates of the Poor Law Institution at Watermoor were able to
hear the service from Canterbury Cathedral on radio sets installed by an anonymous donor. There was a B.B.C. programme from
Cirencester itself in 1935 and a regular column on wireless by
'Rex Radio' and later 'Aerial' began to appear in the Wilts. and
Gloucestershire Standard. The Picture House in the Market Place
moved to the corner of London Road and Victoria Road (now
Bravender House) and in 1937 a new cinema, The Regal, opened
in Lewis Lane on the site of Chester Lodge. It cost £25,000, seated
1,000 people and had a large car park at the rear. In 1927 the
Urban District Council approved plans for the purchase of two
cottages in Silver Street for the installation of public conveni-
ences. The total cost of the enterprise was £1,000. One problem
less easy to solve was the flooding which still occurred periodi-
cally. The town's water system, largely culverted in the central
area, was difficult to manage and in 1929 the filling in of the
canal feeder, the artificial waterway constructed to carry water
from the mill pond on the Churn to the basin of the old Thames
and Severn Canal, was said to have been a contributory cause of
the widespread floods which affected Cirencester in that year,

although a drought followed by heavy rain produced similar conditions in other parts of the country.

The economic depression of the 1920's and 1930's did not leave Cirencester unscathed. In 1921 the Urban District Council reduced the rents of their houses at Chesterton and Watermoor because of the current financial hardship and in 1923 a £10,000 Council Scheme to build Abbey Way, a by-pass at Shepherd's Piece, was embarked upon partly to create employment. The closure of the Midland and South Western Junction Railway works at Watermoor in 1925 and the transfer of the railway to the Great Western Railway two years later meant another loss of jobs. By 1929, 285 men in the town were reported out of work. A few years later the cessation of brewing at the Brewery in Cricklade Street, also caused unemployment. Fears that the Agricultural College might not re-open after its war-time closure and thus add to trading losses, were dispelled following a public appeal for support. In 1923 George V and Queen Mary attended the re–opening ceremony.

The mid-1930's brought a number of celebrations and anniversaries. In 1936 the Urban District Councillors whose numbers had been increased by two in the previous year when the growing district of Stratton had been transferred to the authority, joined in the national commemoration of the centenary of the Municipal Corporations' Act although Cirencester itself had not then achieved borough status. A newly designed chain of office was worn for the first time by the Chairman, George Winstone, at a dinner at the King's Head and a council housing estate at Bowling Green Farm and private estates at Abbey Way and the Mead were officially opened. In 1937 there were again national celebrations for the coronation of George VI. This coincided with a more domestic anniversary in Cirencester – the centenary of the Wilts. and Gloucestershire Standard founded in the same year as the accession of the new King's great-grandmother, Queen Victoria.

Another feature of the twentieth century was the growing influence of the Labour Party. Cirencester's first Labour candidate was Joseph Alpass, a Bristol solicitor who contested the seat in 1918 and in 1924. The Conservatives, however, retained power in the Cirencester and Tewkesbury constituency. From 1929–1959 the Member of Parliament was W.S. Morrison, a Scottish lawyer from a crofting background who rose quickly to ministerial office and served several governments with distinc-

Houses of an earlier period on Cecily Hill   *Courtesy Bingham Library.*

tion. From 1951–9 he was Speaker of the House of Commons and for the last two years of his life from 1959–61, as Viscount Dunrossil, was Governor of Australia.

The fear of war pervaded the later 1930's and Cirencester made preparations for such an emergency. In 1936 at the annual War Office inspection of the local Red Cross detachments, a mock air raid was organised and personnel were warned that they would have to train people to deal with gas attacks. In 1938 volunteers were requested for Air Raid Precaution duties. Normal activities, however, continued. A large housing estate at Chesterton was inaugurated and in the same year, 1938, Professor George Trevelyan came to open the new museum at Abberley House, acquired for the town through the generosity of the Bathurst and Cripps' families who also presented their fine collections of Roman antiquities hitherto housed in private museums.

Within the first week of the declaration of war in September 1939, the first 537 evacuees had arrived – not as many as had been expected. The Wilts. and Gloucestershire Standard reported that 'the children made a sorry procession, clutching teddy bears and dolls, but were surprisingly brave'. A.R.P. emergency shelters were set up and there was a First Aid Post in the Temperance Hall. Ironically the current film being shown at one of the cinemas was George Formby in 'Trouble Brewing'! Black-out material was speedily purchased and made up by Cirencester housewives. Messrs Boultons were selling this at

160

2/6d per yard. In December it was stated that Cirencester had one of the blackest black-outs in the country and after an alarming spate of pedestrian accidents, the Council arranged to place hurricane lamps at danger points. Buildings were requisitioned – including the Bingham Library which found a temporary war-time home in other premises in Dyer Street.

The civilian war effort took many forms – people enrolled as A.R.P. Wardens, Special Constables and as members of other voluntary organisations. In 1940, 120 men answered Anthony Eden's appeal for Local Defence Volunteers (later known as the Home Guard). There were many knitting circles – in October 1940 Countess Bathurst reported that her group had already produced 2,000 garments and knitting replaced book-binding on the curriculum of the Boys' Council School. Pig Clubs were formed and all available land dug up to produce food. A British Restaurant, opened in the Church Hall in Cricklade Street, served over 80,000 mid-day meals between December 1940 and June 1942. A bowl of soup could be purchased for 3d, meat and two veg. cost 8d and a sweet 3d. Railings disappeared from public and private buildings. War Weapons' Weeks raised vast amounts of money for munitions – and the total War Savings for the Urban District Council area came to £2,300,000.

Cirencester men were among the very early casualties – in 1939 three went down with the Royal Oak at Scapa Flow. In 1942, Lord Apsley, heir to Earl Bathurst was killed in a flying accident on active service. Units of the armed forces were stationed in and around the town throughout the war. At one time the Bingham Hall housed men of the Pioneer Corps who were followed by New Zealand foresters engaged on felling trees in Cirencester Park for military use. Units of the Polish air force and Americans, who had a hospital at Deer Park, were among others who came to know the town at this time. German prisoners of war, employed on farms in the neighbourhood, were also a not unfamiliar sight.

In June 1944 the thousands of military vehicles which had been assembled in Cirencester Park, awaiting the D-day offensive, were put to use and within just over a year Cirencester celebrated the ending of the war in Europe and the Far East with the customary street teas, bonfires, sports and dancing, remembering, as only a few years before, those who would not come back and whose names were now added to the war memorial beside the parish church.

Victory Celebrations in the Market Place, 1945.   *Courtesy Corinium Museum.*

The festivities over, Cirencester began to tackle the problems of peace time. Housing was a major priority and by 1947, 100 new houses had been constructed on the Chesterton and new Beeches estates. Over the next few years other developments, both council and private, followed to cope with the demands of an increasing population. Older houses in the central parts of the town were rehabilitated and the Council won a Civic Trust Award for part of The Triangle development, now called St. Clement's Walk. Landmarks such as Abbey House and Ashcroft House disappeared in the 1960's and were replaced by modern flats and houses. More recently sheltered housing schemes for the elderly have been a feature. One of these utilised the former Maltings in Cricklade Street, another is being built on the old Jefferies' Nursery site in Tower Street.

There were changes too in the centre of the town. Dyer Court and the buildings behind were demolished to make way for shops and the Forum Car Park, the latter providing a home for the annual Mop fair, removed from the Market Place in the 1960's. A new Police Station was built and Lewis Lane connected with Dyer Street by North and South Way. Although Cirencester had retained its reputation for a variety of small specialist shops, supermarkets now offer additional shopping facilities.

The Maltings – Ashcroft Road. Entrance.   *Photo. A. Welsford.*

Homeberry House – built on the former Maltings' site.   *Photo. A. Welsford.*

The Beeches Community Centre. *Photo. J. Welsford.*

H.R.H. The Duke of Gloucester and David Viner, Curator at the re-opening of the Corinium Museum in 1974. *Courtesy Corinium Museum.*

In the period since the 1939–45 war the town has acquired more amenities. The Beeches, once the home of the Sewell family, was purchased to provide the Phoenix Community Centre, and in 1965 the Urban District Council bought 23 acres of the Abbey Grounds for the use of the public. More recently St. Michael's Park adjoining Watermoor House has provided additional open space and recreational opportunities. A new museum planned in 1971 to incorporate the 1938 building with the adjacent house and warehouses, was formally opened in 1974 by the Duke of Gloucester and won a European Architectural Heritage Award in 1975. The increased space allowed for the display of the additional Roman and medieval material produced as a result of the programme of the Cirencester Excavation Committee founded in 1959. Until 1976 excavations took place annually and added greatly to knowledge of the town's history. A new library was opened in the Waterloo in 1975 when the responsibility for library provision was taken over by Gloucestershire County Council. The connection with Daniel Bingham is maintained by the Bingham Library Trustees, now Cirencester Town Council. The former brewery buildings behind Cricklade Street were converted into the Brewery Workshops and the Niccol Centre. The latter offers recreational activities for the elderly and musical and dramatic entertainment for all. The Cotswold Sports Centre, whose first buildings (the indoor swimming pool) opened in 1975, provides a great variety of sports' facilities.

Educational provision also changed in the post-war period. Following national legislation, Cirencester was among the first areas in Gloucestershire to adopt a comprehensive system. In 1966 the Boys' and Girls' Secondary Schools, based at Deer Park, were merged with the Grammar School to form Cirencester School. By 1971 this was finally installed in new buildings at the Deer Park, having previously operated both on this site and the former Grammar School in Victoria Road. The vacated Grammar School premises were now the home of the Cirencester County Junior and Infants' Schools, transferred from Lewis Lane, and the newly established Teachers' Centre. A new comprehensive school was opened at Kingshill in 1976. This too had used part of the former Grammar School buildings in the first year of its life. The growing population of Chesterton was catered for in a new primary school there which was established in 1971.

Since the war a number of light industries have been attracted

The Brewery Workshops.   *Photo. A. Welsford.*

Chesterton Primary School.   *Photo. J. Welsford.*

to the area and national and international companies and institutions have made their headquarters at Cirencester. The Love Lane Industrial Estate, which in 1963, was providing employment for some 500, has continued to expand. The Gloucestershire County Survey in 1964 emphasized the importance of the town as a service centre for a large rural area and mentioned the good range of manufacturing enterprises and the growing influence of Swindon as a provider of employment. Cirencester has therefore become an increasingly important business and commercial centre and although the railway station was closed in 1964, accessibility to London via Kemble station and the motorway has made commuting an attractive possibility.

These trends and the boom in the tourist industry have inevitably meant pressure on development space as well as growth in the volume of traffic. Local authorities are faced with the perennial problem of reconciling the insatiable demands of cars and lorries trying to get to and through the town with the need to retain its attraction as a residential, shopping and tourist centre and to preserve its architectural and landscape heritage. In 1963 the Urban District Council commissioned Professor Colin Buchanan to consider the town's traffic problems. His detailed report concluded that 'the problems are extemely difficult and that there is no easy or cheap solution to be had for the asking!'. A partial by-pass on the eastern side of the town was built in 1966 and the completion of the ring road some ten years later means that through traffic can avoid the town centre although there is still congestion at peak periods.

In 1974 as a result of local government re-organisation Cirencester Urban District Council ceased to exist and the administration was divided between two authorities – the Cotswold District Council and Cirencester Town Council. For the first time in its long history the town could have a mayor. In the following year in 1975 Cirencester's citizens revived incidents in that long history in the 'Cirencester 1900' celebrations when the bustling thriving modern town looked back to its antecedents in Roman Corinium.

Part of the Ring Road, with the sports centre on the left.   *Photo. J. Welsford.*

St. Michael's Field.   *Photo. A. Welsford.*

WHAT TO SEE

- Bingham House, Dyer Street – offices of Cirencester Town Council (formerly Bingham Library).

- Bingham Hall, King Street.

- The Beeches – Phoenix Community Centre – Beeches Road.

- St. Clements' Walk (The Triangle Development between Thomas Street, Dollar Street and Coxwell Street).

- Brewery Workshops – Brewery Court, Cricklade Street.

- Niccol Centre – Brewery Court, Cricklade Street.

- Corinium Museum.

Abbreviations

B.A.R.   British Archaeological Reports
Bing. L.   Bingham Library, Cirencester
C.A.H.S.   Cirencester Archaeological and Historical Society
             Newsletter
G.R.O.   Gloucestershire Record Office
T.B.G.A.S.   Transactions of Bristol and Gloucestershire Archaeo-
             logical Society
W. & G.S.   Wilts. and Gloucestershire Standard

Principal Sources

GENERAL

The main histories of Cirencester date from the eighteenth, nineteenth and early twentieth centuries.

Rudder, Samuel *History of Cirencester* 1780, 2nd ed. 1800. Rudder was a printer and bookseller living in Cirencester and his work reflects a contemporary view of the town and society. He also wrote *A New History of Gloucestershire* (1779) which was intended as a revision of Sir Robert Atkyns' *Ancient and Present State of Gloucestershire* (1712). Both these books contain references to Cirencester.

Beecham, Kennet J. *History of Cirencester and the Roman City Corinium* 1887, reprinted Alan Sutton 1978 with an introduction by David Verey. (The later edition has Beecham's notes of 1910). Recent excavations and research have disproved some of Beecham's theories about Roman and medieval Cirencester but his book is extremely informative, particularly for the nineteenth century.

Baddeley, W. St. Clair *A History of Cirencester* 1924. Like Beecham, Baddeley was unable to profit by later research. His book ends at the eighteenth century but W. Scotford Harmer contributed a valuable chapter on 'Cirencester, Past and Present, its old streets and Houses'.

ARCHITECTURE AND TOWN DEVELOPMENT

General
Clifton Taylor, A. *Another Six English Towns* 1984, 11–43.
Leech, R. *Historic Towns in Gloucestershire* 1981.
Reece, R. and Catling, C. *Cirencester: the Development and Buildings of a Cotswold Town* 1975, B.A.R. 12.
Verey, D. *Gloucestershire – The Cotswolds* in The Buildings of England Series, 1979, 2nd edition, 161–187.

Parish Church
Fuller, E.A. *History of Cirencester Parish Church* 1883.
Hill, R.E. *Cirencester Parish Church. An Account of its History and Architecture* 1981.

CHAPTER 1   ROMAN CIRENCESTER

For Iron Age background see Clifford, E. *Bagendon, a Belgic Oppidum*, 1961.
For General Works on the period – McWhirr, A.D. *Roman Gloucestershire* 1981, and Wacher, J.S. *Towns of Roman Britain*, 1975 contain many references to Cirencester. Chapter VII of the latter deals specifically with the town.

Excavations are covered by three major reports published by Cirencester Excavation Committee:
Wacher, J.S. and McWhirr, A.D. *Cirencester Excavations I – Early Roman Occupation at Cirencester* 1982.
McWhirr, A.D., Viner, L. and Wells, C. *Cirencester Excavations II – Romano-British Cemeteries at Cirencester* 1982.
McWhirr, A.D. *Cirencester Excavations III – Houses in Roman Cirencester* 1986.

Interim Reports have been published in the Antiquaries' Journal as follows:
Wacher, J.S. *Cirencester 1960* vol. XLI, 63–71. Wacher, J.S. *Cirencester 1961* vol. XLII, 1–14. Wacher, J.S. *Cirencester 1962* vol. XLIII, 15–26. Wacher, J.S. *Cirencester 1963* vol. XLIV, 9–18. Wacher, J.S. *Cirencester 1964* vol. XLV, 97–110. Brown, P.D.C. and McWhirr, A.D. *Cirencester 1966* vol. XLVII, 185–197. Brown P.D.C., McWhirr, A.D. & Smith D.J. *Cirencester 1967–8* vol.

XLIX, 222–243. McWhirr, A.D. *Cirencester 1969–72* vol. LIII, 191–218. McWhirr, A.D. *Cirencester 1973–6* vol. LVIII, 61–30.

Other reports of excavations include Reece, R. *The Oakley Cottage Romano–British Cemetery*, T.B.G.A.S. vol. 81, 51–72. Reece, R. *The Ashcroft Site*, T.B.G.A.S. vol. 94, 92–100. Rennie, D.M. *Excavations in the Parsonage Field, 1958*, T.B.G.A.S. vol. 90, 64–94. Webster, G. *Cirencester, Dyer Court Excavation, 1957*, T.B.G.A.S. vol. 78, 44–85. Zeepvat, R.J. *Observations in Dyer Street and Market Place*, T.B.G.A.S. vol. 97, 65–73. McWhirr, A. *The Roman Town Plan*, B.A.R. 30, 1976, 5–13 is a summary of knowledge gained by excavations in preceding fifteen years.

For guides to existing remains see Viner, D.J. *Surviving Monuments of Corinium – the Roman Cirencester*, Corinium Museum Publications 1973; Viner, D.J. *The Corinium Trail – A Guide to Roman Cirencester*, Corinium Museum Publications 1980; and Wacher, J.S. *Cirencester Roman Amphitheatre*, Department of the Environment 1981.

Specific topics are dealt with in Buckman, J. and Newmarch, C.H. *Illustrations of the Remains of Roman Art in Cirencester*, London 1850; and Ellis, R. *The Cirencester Word Square*, Corinium Museum Publications 1980.

A stimulating discussion of the relationship of Cirencester to the surrounding area is found in Reece, R. *From Corinion to Cirencester – Models and Misconception*, B.A.R. 30, 1976, 61–79.

CHAPTER 2   SAXONS, DANES AND NORMANS

The last years of Roman Cirencester are considered in Wacher, J.S. *Late Roman Developments*, B.A.R. 30, 1976, 15–18. For archaeological evidence of Anglo-Saxon period see Brown, P.D.C. *Archaeological Evidence for the Anglo-Saxon Period*, B.A.R. 30, 1976, 19–46 and Interim Reports published in the Antiquaries' Journal as follows: Brown, P.D.C. & McWhirr, A.D. *Cirencester 1965*, vol. XLVI, 240–54; and Brown, P.D.C. & McWhirr, A.D. *Cirencester 1966*, vol. XLVII, 185–97.

The problem of the Collegiate Church and the role of Regenbald are discussed in Evans, A.K.B. *The Collegiate Church at Cirencester*, B.A.R. 30, 1976, 46–61. A forthcoming major report from Cirencester Excavation Committee, *Cirencester: Saxon Church and Medieval Abbey* encompasses all the results of recent excavations and research on the Saxon Church.

References are quoted from the G.N. Garmonsway translation of the *Anglo-Saxon Chronicle*, 1953 and the L. Sherley Price translation of Bede. A *History of the English Church and People*, 1968. For place names see Smith, A.H. *The Place Names of Gloucestershire*, 1964.

The hundredal and shire organisation and the Anglo-Saxon status of Cirencester are dealt with in Slater, T. *The Town and its Regions in the Anglo-Saxon and Medieval Periods*, B.A.R. 30, 1976, 81–95.

Finberg, H.P.R. *Gloucestershire Studies 1957 – The Genesis of Gloucestershire Towns*, 54–61 has references to Cirencester in Saxon and early Norman periods.

For the Domesday Survey see Moore, J. (ed. & trans.) *Domesday Book – Gloucestershire*, 1982; Taylor, C.S. *An Analysis of the Domesday Survey of Gloucestershire*, 1889 and Slater, T. op. cit.

CHAPTERS 3 AND 4   MEDIEVAL CIRENCESTER

For history of the Abbey see forthcoming report from Cirencester Excavation Committee *Cirencester: Saxon Church and Medieval Abbey*. Ross, C.D. ed. *The Cartulary of Cirencester Abbey*, vols. I & II 1964. Devine, M. ed. *The Cartulary of Cirencester Abbey*, vol. III 1967. For background of the Augustinian Order Dickinson, J.C. *The Origins of the Augustinian Canons and their Introduction into England*. See also Hunt, R.W. *The Schools and the Cloister. The Life and Writings of Alexander Nequam 1157–1217*, 1984; and Welsford, A. *The Library of St. Mary's Abbey*, C.A.H.S. no. 17, 1975, 4–12.

Descriptions of the medieval town are found in Slater, T. *Town and Region in the Anglo-Saxon and Medieval Periods*, B.A.R. 30,

1976, 97–104; and Fuller, E.A. *Ancient Cirencester and its Streets and Hundreds*, W.& G.S. October 1873. The castle is dealt with in Fuller, E.A. *Cirencester Castle*, T.B.G.A.S. vol. XV, 103–119. The contemporary description of its fate is from *Gesta Stephani*, ed. K.R. Potter 1955.

The status of the inhabitants and their relations with the Abbey are considered in Fuller, E.A. *Tenures of Land in Cirencester*, T.B.G.A.S. vol. II, 285–319; Fuller, E.A. *Cirencester, the Manor and the Town*, T.B.G.A.S vol. IX, 298–344; Fuller, E.A. *Cirencester Guild Merchant*, T.B.G.A.S vol. XVIII, 37–74 and 175–6.

For the Hospitals see Fuller, E.A. *Cirencester Hospitals*, T.B.G.A.S. vol. XVII, 53–62; Fuller, E.A. *The Hospital of St. John*, T.B.G.A.S. vol. VIII, 224–8 and *Victoria County History* vol. II, 1907, 122–3.

The Grammar School is discussed by Fuller, E.A. *Cirencester Free Grammar School*, T.B.G.A.S. vol. XI, 118–129 and T.B.G.A.S. vol. XVII, 59–62.

See also Fuller, E.A. *The Register of the Chapel of the Blessed Virgin Mary in the Parish Church of Cirencester*, T.B.G.A.S. vol. XVIII, 320–331; and for the medieval wool trade Woodman, M. *From Cotswold to Calais*, Corinium Museum Publications 1978.

Street and Place Names: Smith, A.H. *The Place Names of Gloucestershire*, 1964.

CHAPTER 5   TUDOR CIRENCESTER

For fate of the Abbey buildings and the canons Reece, R. *The Abbey of St. Mary, Cirencester*, T.B.G.A.S. vol. 81, 198–203; and Baskerville, G. *The Dispossessed of Gloucestershire*, T.B.G.A.S vol. 49, 63–123.

The recantation of William Phelps is printed in Beecham, 285–7.

Catholics in Cirencester, McGrath, P. *Gloucestershire and the Counter Reformation in the Reign of Elizabeth I*, T.B.G.A.S vol. 88, 5–28.

Puritans in Cirencester Price, F.D. *Commission for Ecclesiastical Causes for the Dioceses of Bristol and Gloucester 1574*, T.B.G.A.S. vol. 59, 61–183.

Details of Members of Parliament are given in Williams, W.R. *Parliamentary History of the County of Gloucestershire 1213–1898*, 1898. The Weavers' Company is dealt with in Harmer, W.S. *History of The Weavers' Company*, undated and for the Grammar School see Fuller, E.A. *op.cit.* in chapters 3 and 4, and Leech, A.F. *Victoria County History* vol. II, 1907, 388–396.

CHAPTER 6
CIRENCESTER IN THE SEVENTEENTH CENTURY

Men and Armour for Gloucestershire in 1608 compiled by John Smith of Nibley, printed 1902.

Details of parish administration – *Cirencester Vestry Book and Churchwardens' Accounts*, G.R.O.

For the Civil War see *Civil War Tracts and Pamphlets Collection*, Bing. L., Jennings, R.W. *The Cotswolds in the Civil War*, Corinium Museum Publications 1976 and Taylor, J.N. *A Cirencester Treasure Trove*, T.B.G.A.S. vol. 79, 177–179.

Details of Members of Parliament – Williams, W.R. *op.cit.* in chapter 5.

Quaker history – Stephens, L. *Cirencester Quakers 1655–1973*, 1973.

Presbyterians – Murch, J. *A History of the Presbyterian and General Baptist Churches*, 1835, 24–34.

General Protestant Dissent – Jones, A.E. *Protestant Dissent in Gloucestershire – a comparison 1676 and 1735*, T.B.G.A.S. vol. 101, 131–147.

Directories referred to are *Baily's Directory*, 1784 and the *Universal British Directory*, 1792.

Copies of *Cirencester Flying Post* are in the Bingham L. and Gloucester City Library. See also Black, J. *The Cirencester Flying Post*, C.A.H.S. no. 25, 1983, 5–19, and Norris, H.E. *Printers and Booksellers of Cirencester*, 1912. *The Account Books of Timothy Stevens*, are in the Gloucester City Library and on microfilm in Bingham Library.

Transport – Paine, M.J. *Turnpike Trusts of Cirencester*, 1967, G.R.O. Hartland, J. *The Historical Development of the Cirencester–Stroud Road*, C.A.H.S. no. 26, 1984. Household, H. *The Thames and Severn Canal*, 1969. Viner, D.J. *The Thames and Severn Canal in Cirencester*, B.A.R. 30, 1976, 126–145.

Correspondence between Richard and George Cumberland is printed in Black, C. ed. *The Cumberland Letters 1718–1784*, 1912.

The Bathurst family, Cirencester House and Park – Bathurst, A.B. *The History of the Apsley and Bathurst Families*, 1903. Lees-Milne, J. *Earls of Creation*, 1962. Martin, P. *Pursuing Innocent Pleasures – The Gardening World of Alexander Pope*, 1984. Whitehead, P. *Cirencester Park – Historical Portraits and Family Possessions*, 1957.

Parliamentary affairs – Jennings, R.W. *The Cirencester Contest*, T.B.G.A.S vol. 92, 157–169 and Williams, W.R. op. cit. in chapter 5.

For the Rev. Samuel Johnson see Jennings, R.W. *The Sad Story of the Reverend Samuel Johnson*, C.A.H.S. no. 16, 1974, 4–14.

Parish and poor law administration – *Parish Vestry Book, Churchwardens' Accounts* and *Records of Overseers of the Poor*, G.R.O.

Blue and Yellow Schools' Records, G.R.O. Life of Rebecca Powell – Barker, J. *William and Rebecca George (Powell) and* their *Town House, now Gloucester House*, B.A.R. 30, 1976, 113–126.

Charities – *Report of the Charity Commissioners for Gloucestershire 1819–1837*, 1890, 382–424.

Apprentice lists – *The Cirencester Society in London*, 1953.

Theatre – Denning, D.A. *Early Theatricals at Cirencester*, C.A.H.S. no. 14, 1972.

Book Clubs – Kaufmann, P. *A Bookseller's Record of Eighteenth Century Book Clubs*, 1966.

CHAPTER 8
CIRENCESTER IN THE EARLY NINETEENTH CENTURY

Poll Books for 1790, 1802, 1812, Bing. L. *Churchwardens' Accounts and Overseers of the Poor Records*, G.R.O.
The Gibbs' Family Papers, Bing. L.
Cirencester 'Gleaner' for year 1816, Bing. L.
Cirencester Savings' Bank Records, Bing. L.
Minutes of Cirencester Town Commissioners and Cirencester Board of Guardians, G.R.O.
Plans of Cirencester – Hall, Richard & Sons, 1793 and Wood, John, 1835, Bing. L.
Slater, T. *Family, Society and the Ornamental Villa on the Fringes of the English Country Town*, Journal of Historical Geography, 4, 1978, 128–144. Slater, T. *Estate Ownership and Nineteenth Century Suburban Development*, B.A.R. 30, 1976, 145–158.
Diary of Margaret Ann Croome, G.R.O.
Cirencester Permanent Library – Minute Book, Bing. L.

CHAPTER 9   VICTORIAN CIRENCESTER

Slater, T. *The Cirencester Improved Dwellings Company 1880–1914*, B.A.R. 30, 1976, 171–198.
Beecham, A. *An Essay in Family History*, 1981, Bing. L.
Jefferies, R. *Hodge and his Masters*, 1880.

Minutes of Cirencester Town Commissioners and Local Government Board, G.R.O.

Cirencester School of Art Records, Bing. L. and G.R.O.

Mechanics Institute Records, Bing. L. Cirencester Permanent Library Minute Books, Bing. L. Jennings, R.W. The Revd. W.F. Powell and the Restoration of Cirencester Parish Church, B.A.R. 30, 1976, 158–168.

Hibbert and Richardson, The Water Supply of Cirencester – a paper read to Cotswold Naturalist and Archaeological Society 1912.

Elliott, J.W. History and Description of Cirencester Water Undertaking 1882–1956, 1956. Wilts. and Gloucestershire Standard – numerous references from 1837 onwards.

Census Enumerators' Returns 1851, 1861, 1871, 1881.

CHAPTER 10   CIRENCESTER IN THE TWENTIETH CENTURY

Cirencester Child Care Committee Records, Bing. L. Cirencester Board of Guardians – Paupers' Lists 1901–1912, Bing. L. Bingham Library Records, Bing. L. Beecham, K.J. Plan of Cirencester in 1911. Hughes, D.A. History of Cirencester Urban District Council, published in Wilts. and Gloucestershire Standard July 1973–April 1974. Figes, E. Little Eden – A Child at War, 1978 (a personal view of the town during the early years of the 1939–45 war). Anderson, R. A Survey of Waterways with reference to the Flood of 1929, 1931. Buchanan, C. Traffic in Cirencester. A Brief for the Re-development of the Town, 1964. Conservation in Cirencester, 1970, pub. Cirencester Urban District Council. Waring, D. Conservation in Cirencester, B.A.R. 30, 1976, 198–200. Gloucestershire Quinquennial Review – Cirencester Town Map Area – Survey 1958 and 1960 – Cirencester Town Map – 2nd Review 1968 and 1970.

Selective Index

Abbey 28, **29**, 31ff, 49ff, 60, 62ff, 65, 66, **66**
Abbey house **36**, 78f, 100f
Abbots 31, 38, 42ff, 52, 54, 60ff
Amphitheatre 10, 21, **22**, 103
Apsley – see Bathurst
Ashcroft 122, 129, 147, **149**, 157, 162, **163**

Banks 89, 114f
Barton 17, 21, 25, 26, 40, **41**, 43, 79, 97, 138
Bathurst
    Estate 26, 66, 78, 86, 95, 97, 98, **98**, **99**,
       100, 138, 145
    Family 86, 95, **95**, 96, **96**, 103, 117, 129,
       136, 137, 140, 151, 161
Beecham, John **53**, 78, 142, **143**
Beeches 16, **16**, 162, **164**, 165
Bingham, D.G. 153, 154
Bingham Hall 154, 156, **158**, 161
Bingham Library – see Libraries

Canal – see Transport
Carriers – see Transport
Castle 35, 45
Chapels – see Churches
Charities 67, 68, 76, 104, **113**, 134, 153
Chester-Master – see Master
Chesterton 4, 25, 28, 34, 48, 128, 157, 160
Christianity 11, **14** – see also Churches
Churches
    Parish 37, 55, **58**, 60ff, **61**, **62**, **63**, 68, 69,
       101, 103, 134, 147
    Other 23, 24, 28, 68, 69, 82ff, 102, 103,
       147, **148**, 149, **149**
Cirencester House see Bathurst
Cirencester Park see Bathurst
Civil war 74ff, **78**, **80**
Corn Hall 129, **130**, **144**, 145, 147, 154
Cripps' family 4, 89, 101, 103, 107, 112,
    114, 115, 122, 132, 136, 140

Danvers, Sir John, 66, 70ff
Dissenters – see Churches
Dobunni 1, 4, 11
Domesday survey 25ff

Entertainments 107, **124**, 144, 145, **146**,
    147, 154f, 159

Fairs 43, 116, 145, 162

Guilds – Merchant 54, 71
    Trinity 52

Weavers' 70, 76

Inns 93, **93**, 112, 116, 129, 130, 145

Law and Order 39, 40, 50, 104f, 117f, **148**,
    149, 162
Libraries 42, 52, 65, **111**, 123, 142, 145,
    153, 154, 161, 165
Local Government 25f, 39, 51f, 66, 70, 84,
    118, **137**, 138, **139**, 140, 141, 167
Lovelace 86

Manor – see Local Government
Mansion – see Bathurst
Manufactures
    Agricultural 132, 151
    Carriage works 132
    Edge-tools 112, 132
    Foundries 132
    Railway carriage works 132
    Other 74, 110, 112, 132, 167
Market place 46, 50f, 54, 78, 90, 112, **119**,
    120, **130**, 145
Markets 7, 17, 28, 34, 42, 48, 89, 112, 129
Master 66, 73, 78, 85, 100, 127, 140
Militia 77, 115, 149, 150, 157, **157**, 161f
Mills 26, 28, 43, **48**, 50, 63f, **64**, 88, 100f,
    132
Museums 123, 136, 160, **164**, 165

Nequam, Alexander 42, 43
Newspapers 90, **90**, 91, 160

Oakley Grove 95 – see also Bathurst
Oakley Hall 96 – see also Bathurst
Oakley Manor – see Bathurst

Parliament 70, 85, 94, 100f, 115, 120, 140,
    151, 154, 159
Police – see Law and Order
Poor 76, 103, 112, 115, 120, **120**, 134, 153,
    158
Population 48, 72, **75**, 110, 127, **133**
Powell, Rebecca 104, **106**
Public health 103, 127, 138
Public houses – see Inns
Public utilities
    Electricity 157
    Gas 120
    Water 138, 140, 157

Querns 48, 50f

179